PLUMBERS
IN
UNITY

PLUMBERS
IN
UNITY

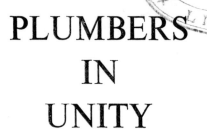

HISTORY OF THE
PLUMBING TRADES UNION
1865-1965

J. O. French

A1

Co-operative Printing Society Ltd., Tudor Street, E.C.4
Manchester and Newcastle.

" That no one but the trade of plumbers shall meddle with works touching such trade, except by the assent of the best and most skilled men of the said trade, testifying that he knows how well and lawfully to do his work, so that the said trade shall not be scandalised or the commonalty damaged and deceived by folks who do not know their trade."

Ordinance issued by the Worshipful Company of Plumbers in 1365.

CONTENTS

LIST OF ILLUSTRATIONS

FOREWORD

The craft of plumbing is not the oldest profession. That distinction is universally acknowledged to belong to an occupation which is concerned more with entertainment than with the promotion of health and hygiene.

Nevertheless, the roots of plumbing lie very deep indeed. It can be traced with assurance to the early Mediterranean civilisations of the Egyptians, Greeks and Romans: indeed, the latter were responsible for its introduction into Britain nearly two thousand years ago. Man cannot exist without water. From the time he first cohabited with others to form a primitive community, there has been the need to convey water from its natural sources to the communal site.

Students of the plumbing craft will find abundant material on its origins and development and much will be found interesting and entertaining even by the layman. This work is not intended to be a history of plumbing. Nor is it our intention to delve into the origins of trade unionism—a subject on which an even more copious supply of literature is available for those wishing to examine the evolution of working-class associations at home or abroad.

Our primary objective is to follow the growth of the Plumbing Trades' Union since its establishment as a national organisation just a century ago. No attempt is made to pass judgment, to analyse, to dissect or to prophesy. From the material at our disposal—often rather limited and incomplete —we have tried to set down in an uncomplicated manner the main domestic events in the first hundred years of our organisation's existence.

If readers will accept the definition and limitations described they will need no apology for the obvious omissions and restrictions which could be regarded as reprehensible in a more ambitious project.

PLUMBERS IN UNITY

CHAPTER I

1800-1865: THE DAYS OF PERSECUTION

NOT until the repeal of the Combination Acts in 1824-25 were trade unions, as defined by the Webbs*, permitted to function in Britain with impunity. The Combination Acts, passed in 1799 and 1800 by a Parliament under the domination of a new class of profit-hungry industrialists, and still trembling at the recollection of recent events across the Channel, forbade all combinations of workmen and decreed heavy sentences for transgressors.

Any student of British working-class history will be familiar with the tyranny and oppression committed under these infamous Acts. Let it be sufficient for us to quote a short passage from Raymond Postgate's book *The Builders' History*—a work to which we shall make many further references before our final page is reached. Speaking of the 25-year period during which the Combination Acts were in force, Postgate says:

" Case after case exists of unions brought into the open by a prosecution under the Acts and forced to dissolve, while its active members were punished by sentences of imprisonment running sometimes into years. Such punishments—which included public whippings—were awarded even in cases where the employers had connived at and welcomed the journeymen's associations; where any resistance had been made to the encroachments of the unscrupulous new employers the penalties were even more severe. The compositors on *The Times* were prosecuted in 1810 for belonging to a combination, and in sentencing them to periods of imprisonment varying from nine months to two years, Sir John Silvester—known as Bloody Black Jack—said ' Prisoners, you have been convicted of a most wicked conspiracy to injure the most vital interests of those very employers who gave you bread, with intent to impede and injure them in their business; and indeed as far as in you lay to effect their ruin. The

---

* *A trade union is a continuous association of wage-earners for the purpose of maintaining or improving the conditions of their employment.*

B

frequency of such crimes among men of your class of life and their mischievous and dangerous tendency to ruin the fortunes of those employers which a principle of gratitude and self-interest should induce you to support, demand of the law that a severe example should be made of those persons who shall be convicted of such daring and flagitious combinations in defiance of public justice and in violation of public order. No symptom of contrition on your part has appeared—no abatement of the combination in which you are accomplices has yet resulted from the example of your convictions'."

The remarks of " Bloody Black Jack " Silvester deserve to be read twice. They reflect something of the incredible state of mind of the British ruling class in the early nineteenth century and the degree of contempt in which the working class was held.

At the beginning of the last century it is therefore obvious that there was not the least encouragement for a working man to pursue his convictions and join with his mates in common purpose against his employer in order to improve the deplorable rates of pay and conditions of labour. It is, indeed, quite remarkable that associations of working men did survive at all in such circumstances. The Webbs attribute this to three factors: the extremely inefficient organisation of the police, the absence of any public prosecutor, and (in many cases) the acceptance of combinations of workmen by the more enlightened employers. Nevertheless, the threat of discovery and subsequent prosecution was always present.

Unfortunately, the sacrifices of these few brave men who decided, against all odds, to keep their self-respect and integrity are too often forgotten—not only by the general public *but by the modern trade union member as well*. For the working classes in particular it would surely be more appropriate to accord to those early martyrs at least the same measure of respect and reverence as is given so unreservedly to our heroes of the battlefield.

In spite of the undisguised malevolence of the legislature, however, the spirit of unity against iniquity was indestructible. As the Romans failed to wipe out Christianity, and the Nazis failed to a lesser degree in a much shorter period to exterminate the Jews, so the British ruling classes in the first

two decades of the nineteenth century were so utterly unsuccessful in their efforts to extinguish the flame of trade
unionism that less than one year after the repeal of the
Combination Acts, Buckingham Palace itself was " blacked "
by journeymen carpenters and work was only resumed after
the active intervention of the Coldstream Guards. This,
incidentally, was *not* the occasion when Queen Victoria said
" We are not amused;" George IV was on the throne at the
time and his comments on the clash between bayonets and
wood chisels are not recorded—and even if they were, they
would probably be unintelligible.

The man primarily responsible for the repeal of the
Combination Acts in 1824-25 was a London tailor, Francis
Place. Appropriately enough, he was a " member in
business " who had previously been a journeyman and had
not forgotten his sufferings and indignities as a leather
breeches maker. After years of patient campaigning he
finally succeeded in promoting a Parliamentary Bill aimed
at the repeal of the Combination Acts. This, amid such
confusion and political absurdity, was finally resolved into
three separate Bills which passed through the House of
Commons and later through the House of Lords.

Only after the Bills had become law did the legislature
appreciate vaguely what it had done. The ridiculous manner
in which trade unions were legalised in Britain by what must
surely have been one of the most incompetent British Parlia-
ments of all time is described by Francis Place himself in an
unpublished autobiography, quoted extensively by Raymond
Postgate. By comparison, the exploits of the Keystone Cops
or the Marx Brothers seem quite pedestrian.

The conclusion of this tragi-comedy was the signal for an
immediate upsurge of organised labour. Many modern trade
unions trace their origins from this point—perhaps for the
only reason that records of earlier associations of journeymen
were either non-existent or failed to survive the period before
1825, when they could be used as evidence of conspiracy.
It is therefore appropriate that we should turn from the
general scene of trade unionism in the shameful times of the
Combination Acts to the first indications that plumbers, too,
were conscious of the need for unity.

THE FIRST YEARS OF " FREEDOM "

Local societies of plumbers existed before 1800. There is evidence that Francis Place had drafted rules for such societies in 1795 or thereabouts. Organisation among journeymen plumbers at that time, however—and indeed, for many years to come—was restricted to the North of England where the force of the Industrial Revolution was having the greatest impact on the working class. As we have already pointed out at the beginning of this book, we do not intend to speculate on the possibility of some national link between local plumbers' societies in the early 1800's. No doubt the exercise would be an absorbing one if attempted—but the documents are lacking and the search would not be justified. Once again we are content to rely on the testimony of Raymond Postgate, who declares: " The Operative Plumbers appear to have existed as a national society in 1831 (Plumbers' Rules, 1846, and Cashbook). This Society only covered the North of England. An attempt was made, at the suggestion of the master plumbers, to organise London plumbers at the beginning of 1834, against the master builders, but the society disappeared in the general debacle."

Certainly there is indisputable evidence that the Operative Plumbers and Glaziers Society was one of the several building trade unions which combined to form the first federal association of individual unions, the Operative Builders' Union. Postgate declares: " In 1832 the Operative Builders' Union, formed probably by a federation of existing unions, comes into prominence, and by its activities turns small feeble societies into one national body, powerful in its great membership and careful organisation. In every town that it entered, it brought an inrush of new members. The Plumbers in Manchester enrolled in the first eighteen months of their existence seven new members. In the six months after they joined the general Union they enrolled 58."

The policy, finances and rules of the O.B.U. were decided every six months by delegates from all seven member unions, who assembled in the Grand Lodge or " Builders' Parliament." Each craft section maintained autonomy over its own development, although there was co-ordination at district and local level. In short, the O.B.U. was in many respects similar to the present National Federation of Building Trades Operatives—at least, insofar as it attempted to secure concerted policies and action for the affiliated societies.

More than thirty years after the heyday of the O.B.U., one particular feature of its constitution was embodied in the structure of certain trade unions, including our own. This was the practice of moving the " seat of government " (Executive headquarters) from one town to another. We retained this feature until 1921, when on the instruction of the 1919 Delegate Meeting the Union set up permanent headquarters in London. Raymond Postgate also records that it was " retained with other rules by the General Union of Carpenters and Joiners right up till its absorption in 1921, and for many years also by the Bricklayers (Manchester Order)."

The catalyst which led to the decline and subsequent extinction of the O.B.U. was the opposition to the introduction into the building industry of the system of general contracting. The operatives were apparently intoxicated by initial successes and became reckless. The storm broke in Manchester in 1833. " The masters were ready to fight," says Raymond Postgate, " not merely because they saw a chance of destroying the union, but because they had found that they could not kill the system of general contracting. ' Persons and public bodies ' would not enter into separate contracts for plastering, joinery and so on. To this demand of the men was added, where necessary, the demand for the expulsion of blacklegs. Both of these were demands consciously aimed at the control of industry, and enforced by the threat that if they were not conceded, the operatives would offer the public direct labour. To these were added, from place to place, certain detail demands, not always presented in the most tactful or reasonable way. . . ."

The masters' response to the building workers' demands was " the document." This was a sentence destined to become notorious in the annals of British trade unionism, and read as follows. " We, the undersigned . . . do hereby declare that we are not in any way connected with the General Union of the Building Trades and that we do not and will not contribute to the support of such members of the said union as are or may be out of work in consequence of belonging to such union." The date was 15th June, 1833.

Virtually all large building operations in Lancashire ceased for the ensuing three months. During that time, the strike spread to Birmingham. Simultaneously, Robert Owen (pioneer of the Co-operative Movement) was drawing up his plans for the establishment of a " Grand National Guild of Builders " which would give the public direct labour as well as providing medical, educational, banking and other services to its members. He also fanned the fire of dispute by persuading building workers to press a demand for an eight-hour day. The strike dragged on into October and November.

As a result of dwindling finances in the various societies, section by section the workers bitterly accepted defeat and signed the "document." Meanwhile, Robert Owen was promoting the inception of yet another massive federal body of which the O.B.U. itself was to form only a part. This was the Grand National Consolidated Trades Union, inaugurated in February 1834. It astounded the critics by claiming a membership of half a million within the first few months of its existence—even without the support of the O.B.U. In his book *Foes to Tyranny* Mr. W. S. Hilton (N.F.B.T.O. Research Officer) points out that " in fact, the Grand National had not performed any recruiting miracle among the unorganised. Its membership was achieved, in the main, by the simple amalgamation of the already existing trade unions which gave it their allegiance. And even then, knowing the relatively small membership of some of the strongest unions within the country, it is very doubtful if the figure of half a million was anywhere near the truth."

The meteoric rise of the Grand National Consolidated was as short-lived as a threepenny rocket on Guy Fawkes' night. It had no common policy and it emphasised rather than eliminated the weaknesses of its member societies. Its management was corrupt, its Executive incompetent and its administration inefficient. Disaster overtook it in March 1834, when some of its agricultural delegates—later to become immortalised as the " Tolpuddle Martyrs "—were sentenced to seven years' transportation for administering illegal oaths.

The Grand National was wound up in August 1834, having brought little but discredit to the trade union movement.

More regrettable is the fact that the Grand National Consolidated was largely responsible for the death of the building workers' compact and well organised federation, the O.B.U. The novelty of the Grand National, coupled with Owen's inspired visions of a new society, seduced many local societies away from the O.B.U., so inflicting the *coup de grace* on a body already mortally wounded by the protracted industrial struggle. Its final stand was made in London: building operatives employed by Cubitt's boycotted the beer of Combe, Delafield & Company, who refused to employ trade unionists. Cubitt's retaliated and supported the brewers by taking none but their beer into the building yards and shops. The men, still defiant, were locked out—and remained so for three months. The end of the O.B.U. came in September 1834, when the secretary of the masons' section (anticipating the inevitable) absconded with a substantial part of the remaining funds. Robert Owen's dreams, so far as the building workers were concerned, lay shattered in the wreckage of federations.

EARLY ASSOCIATIONS OF PLUMBERS

And what of the Plumbers? Raymond Postgate tells us that after the debacle of 1834 " the Plumbers' national society —O.P.G.—in Manchester recorded very few entries . . . and its membership figures for the Manchester 1 Lodge fell from 85 to 48. That they did not fall farther was due to the efforts of a small group of men, led by Arthur Higgins and another Robert Owen, who continually took upon themselves the hard work of reorganisation which everyone else shrank from." The general impression remains that the " national " society disintegrated into autonomous local plumbers' societies, operating independently of one another and paying no more than lip service to the larger organisation that nominally survived.

In spite of the disasters of the 1830's, however, trade unionism was now firmly and irrevocably established in Britain as part of the industrial situation, although thousands of masters still refused to believe it. Licking their wounds, several societies began to reassemble their ranks and strengthen their finances and organisation. Among them were the plumbers.

From notes made by Sidney Webb (author of *The History of Trade Unionism*) we have evidence that some form of national organisation was functioning in 1839 under the title " Operative Plumbers and Glaziers." This may well be the Manchester society mentioned by Raymond Postgate. Positive information on this period is extremely scarce: in fact, our only confirmation of the existence of a national union during the years 1839 to 1849 lies in the printed Code of Laws as revised at a Special Delegate Meeting of the " Operative Plumbers' Trade and Provident Association " held in Liverpool on 26th and 27th December, 1849. In his introduction the Corresponding Secretary, James Carter McDermott, declares: " A very strict inquiry into the state of the Association has recently taken place, and most strenuous efforts have been made to place it on a firm and stable footing. The Laws are framed with a view of affording the utmost advantages to its members, consistent with the contributions paid. And the experience of the last thirteen years will have the effect of directing the future operations of the society with prudence, and due regard for the interests of members and their employers." We shall have a little more to say about this Association later on.

Other scraps of information, here and there, give us tantalising glimpses of local societies of plumbers during this period. In 1836, for example, the Liverpool Plumbers' Society had 33 members who paid a monthly contribution of 1s. 3d. each. Numbers fell to 20 in 1842, but recovered well in later years and reached a total of 56 in 1858. This particular local society survived in its original form until 1862, when a committee was formed to alter the rules and transform the Society into a " tontine " club known as the " Friendly, Sick and Burial Society." Funds of the earlier association were divided equally among the members except for the sum of 13s. per head, which was retained as each member's entrance fee into the new organisation. Total receipts for the year 1871 were £101 5s.: after deductions for expenses, the sum of £81 3s. 6d. was shared among 35 members.

Featuring more prominently than any other city in the records of our Union is Manchester. In fact, with all due respect to Geordies, Scots, Irishmen, Cockneys, Welshmen and others, it has to be admitted that every effort to trace the source of a national brotherhood of plumbing craftsmen leads back to Manchester. It may be that through lack of information we are being less than fair to other Lanchashire towns, notably Preston, Blackburn, Liverpool and Rochdale, which in all probability had their own local plumbers' societies in the early nineteenth century. Nevertheless, our earliest documents mainly concern Manchester. We think there may be some merit in leaving the chronological sequence of events for a page or two and examining some of the ancient records of Manchester societies still in our possession.

In point of fact, the more closely we scrutinise these the more difficult it becomes to distinguish between what might have been a " national " society with headquarters in Manchester and a purely local society (or Lodge) of plumbers. This difficulty is mentioned in Raymond Postgate's comments on the plumbers' organisation during the years 1845-46: " The Operative Plumbers and Glaziers, the national union whose headquarters were in Manchester, was well on the way to recovery. It does not seem that the Society extended much beyond the North of England; with the exception of one entry of money from London and of a Birmingham Lodge, we hear only of Lodges at " Rochdale, Liverpool, Halifax, Blackburn, Sheffield, Bel's oth Barn," etc. The Plumbers alone of building unions certainly joined the National Association [of United Trades] and levied themselves for its support. They had a membership of about 1,000—not so very small, considering that plumbing is not a large trade. They enforced a rule expelling any member taking piecework. Their internal organisation seems to have been much like that of the Masons. The " seat of government " had much less tendency to move: it had been at Rochdale in 1837, but for the next 14 years remained in Manchester. Otherwise they retained many of the characteristics of Trade Unionism before Owen's day, including ale-drinking. (" 1845. May 10. Committee's drink 15s. 6d. Officers' drink 12s." If this was beer at 2d. a pint it seems to show plumbing was a thirsty trade, for the rules . . . provided that " no person of idle or dissipated habits can be admitted a member of this Association."). It is not possible to disentangle, by the records, the finances of the Manchester Lodge from those of the Society as a whole, but it appears that in this year [1845] the Lodge had a reserve fund of £122, which seemed to it a sum justifying immediate forward action."

Confusion is further confounded by the fact that the " Operative Plumbers' Trade and Provident Association," mentioned earlier, and claiming unbroken existence from at least 1836, appeared to be centred in Birmingham. Certainly the secretary, James C. McDermott, was the Birmingham representative at a Special Delegate Meeting held in Liverpool in 1849 for the revision of the rules. Moreover, there is no doubt that this Association could equally claim to be a " national " one as distinct from a local society, since the names of the Committee appointed " to revise and amend the general laws " are printed at the beginning of the rule book containing McDermott's address, part of which we have previously quoted. Other members of that Committee were : William Stephenson, Liverpool (Chairman); Robert Jopson (Bury); Thomas Clarkson (Bradford); Thomas Norton (Sheffield); Joseph Mitchell (Bristol), and Frederick Foue (Liverpool).

It is possible, of course, that this Society and the one in Manchester were either two independent " national " organisations, or two parts of a single association. The fact that one of our early General Secretaries, George Cherry, referred in his 1895 report to the Liverpool Delegate Meeting as representative of 14 Lodges " including Birmingham and Manchester " seems to substantiate the latter of the two possibilities; and, as we shall see later on, Raymond Postgate also leans in this direction. It is most unlikely that two separate " national " societies should hold Delegate Meetings in the same town in the same year.

No clear solution to the mystery of relationships between plumbers' societies in the mid-nineteenth century can be formulated. Events in the building trade in 1845-46, however, are of some significance. Raymond Postgate asserts that " it was the ill-advised confidence of the Plumbers, it would appear, that precipitated the offensive of 1846." Our own records certainly confirm his account of the activities of the Manchester Society in 1845, when they resolved to campaign for a reduction in the number of apprentices permitted to each employer. Many of our members will recognise this theme, which, in different terms, has occupied the attention of plumbers through the years right down to the present day. On May Day, 1845, it was "proposed and seconded that the *Manchester Advertiser* prints the address to be issued to the Masters of Manchester and Salford." At the same meeting, it was proposed, seconded and agreed " that the persons deputed to wait upon the masters with the address, if any questions be asked, to be answered as follows: that is, any master keeping three men regular winter and summer be allowed to apprentices and any Master beginning business to be Master 12 months before he be allowed one apprentice."

Further justification for the claim of the Manchester Society to be a "national" one appears in the record on 28th June, when it is minuted that "Bailey Smith be not admitted into this Society and that a letter be wrote to Ashton Lodge respecting the same," and that "James Haywood and Arthur Higgins be the Delegates to open the Lodge at Oldham and that they receive the sum of 7s. 6d. each for their expenses for the same." Later, on 9th August, it was agreed that "the case of Macclesfield strike be postponed until we hear the condition of the other Lodges."

During the summer months of 1845, negotiations with the employers made little headway. On 6th September it is minuted: "That there be a General Meeting called on Monday the 8th of September respecting a strike for wages and apprentices and against working for any builders finding their own lead, glass or any other Materials belonging to our trade." The standard craft rate of pay in Manchester at this time, incidentally, was about 27s. a week.

The Manchester Society then decided to approach the Bricklayers, Masons and other trades to find out " whether they will support us." Raymond Postgate records that favourable replies were received from the Bricklayers, Joiners and Painters, and eventually the Masons' Central Committee in

Liverpool also acceded to the plumbers' demand for a general building strike, " one trade coming out after another in an order and on occasions to be decided." The Masons, however, in common with certain other unions, were more concerned with the issue of a nine-hour day. Once again we can discern the fatal chink in the armour of the organised building workers: unity of action had been endorsed, but unity of purpose was singularly lacking.

Their confidence inflated by the promised support, the Manchester plumbers persisted in demanding replies from the Masters to their resolution. On 30th December, 1845, it was agreed " that the former resolution respecting the number of apprentices do stand to commence from this date that any Master infringing on the said rule and that the said members in their employ belonging to this Society do strike the shop."

The conflict began with a number of small victories for the Manchester Society, who paid no strike benefit until February 1846. Even so, it was soon found necessary to raise additional funds by levies on members remaining in employment. Until the end of March, however, the operatives remained confident that they would achieve their aims in full. Then the Masters hardened, and played their two trump cards. First, they locked out every building worker of every craft in south Lancashire: subsequently, they presented a revised form of the infamous " document " of 1833.

" Before the month of April was out," says Raymond Postgate, " the painters, who had no national organisation to support them, were streaming back to work, followed by the joiners, whose General Union seems to have been unable to control or support them. The battle was not entirely lost, however; the Masons, Bricklayers, Plumbers, Plasterers and Labourers formed a block that it was not easy to move, while an attempt to present the Document in Birmingham was defeated within 48 hours by united lightning action. Funds were in a tolerably good condition: for 3,000 men locked out in Liverpool all but 800 found work elsewhere."

As we mentioned earlier, the issues at stake were by no means confined to the desire of the plumbers to regulate the number of apprentices in relation to journeymen. In accepting the plumbers' overtures in the previous September, the Masons had come out solidly in favour of a demand for a nine-hour day. In joint negotiations which took place on 27th May, 1846—nearly two months after the lock-out had begun—the operatives withdrew their demand in response to a compromise settlement offered by the Masters, who expressed themselves satisfied with the workers' assurances that only labourers belonged to the National Association of United Trades. This body, another general federation of unions which was particularly active among building operatives, was prominent only during the years 1845-46, although it had clearly been regarded by the Masters as a revival of Robert Owen's earlier monstrosity, the Grand National Consolidated. The National Association had been supported by the Manchester Plumbers, who joined in March 1846 and severed their connection in June 1847.

The only Society to win tangible benefits for its members from the 1846 dispute (a wage increase of a shilling a week and a half-hour tea break) was the Masons. Postgate describes the aftermath in the Manchester Operative Plumbers Society: " The Plumbers had received less satisfaction from the settlement, which had not dealt with apprentices. They determined, in spite of their representatives' signature to the terms, to continue the struggle—most unwisely, for their funds were already exhausted, and they would not have been able to carry on as long as they had but for the generosity of the landlord of the public-house where the central committee met, a Mr. Whitehead. They had spent in Manchester already £600 and he had lent them another £95. They carried on as best they could until September, when their debt had risen to £142. They then accepted the fact that the strike had failed, and attempted to pull the society together. It was too late: it had fallen to pieces. Plumbers outside Manchester were not inclined to join an old-fashioned union that was burdened with debt. Mr. Whitehead was still waiting for his original £95 in 1848, and in 1849 a stormy conference of the union was held in Liverpool. Only fourteen lodges composed the society, and a fierce quarrel over finance divided them. Halfway through the conference those who held that the only way to revive the association was by lowering sub-

scriptions, broke away and announced that their Lodges would
reconstitute themselves as local societies. The remaining
delegates decided that they could not support the burden
of the debt and dissolved the society. Manchester accepted
the inevitable, and resolved ' This society recommended as
a Manchester society on 13th July, 1850 '."

So ended yet another decade—and yet another " national "
society of plumbers. As a postscript it is interesting to note
that in spite of the possible existence of a rival " national "
society in Birmingham, the Manchester Society sent two delegates to that town in December 1845 " to open the Lodge
and take things requisite for opening the same, and that they
be allowed 10s. each per day along with the coach fare."
Similar journeys were made to Blackburn (February 1845),
Oldham (June 1845), and to Leicester as late as January 1847.
Correspondence was also being exchanged with " the
Plumbers of Edinburgh and Leith."

THE YEARS OF REVIVAL

Notwithstanding the disaster of 1846 and the Society's
dissolution in 1849, Manchester plumbers were resilient
enough to become active again within a relatively short time.
In 1851 came a move to strengthen organisation in the city
itself. In our possession is a minute book of 1852 containing
an historic preface from the secretary of one of the two Manchester Lodges then existing, James Taylor. If for no other
reason, we are eternally grateful to Mr. Taylor for setting
down so neatly and laboriously (the original spelling is almost
embarrassing in its reflection of the painful process of Mr.
Taylor's composition) an illuminating summary of events of
earlier years. The full text of his preface (with amended
spelling) is reproduced as Appendix 1 at the end of this book.

His opening assertion is encouraging to those of us looking
for continuous organisation to the early nineteenth century.
" A Society of Operative Plumbers and Glaziers has been in
existence in Manchester for upwards of half a century."
More important, however, is the revelation that in 1851 the
two Manchester Lodges, survivors of the Operative Plumbers
and Glaziers of the 1840s, were working once more towards
unity—and towards expansion. It may well be that here

lie the seeds of what was to become the first truly national organisation some fourteen years later.

Our surviving records of the period 1850-1865, while not entirely useless, offer little information of much value. When working on *The History of Trade Unionism,* the Webbs presumably had access to documents beyond our reach; they mention, for example, an old minute book of the Liverpool Plumbers' Society dated 1858, when contributions were recorded as 2s. a month—1s. 6d. for sickness and 6d. for death benefit. Mr. Webb commented: " The minutes are very meagre, containing little more than the election of officers, imposition of fines and granting of benefits—no trade matters at all."

The only source of hard information is the Annual Report of the Operative Plumbers Trade and Provident Society, dated 31st March, 1852, and issued from Birmingham. This is the society referred to before, which sent James McDermott to the 1849 Delegate Meeting in Liverpool. The annual report reveals that the society had declined considerably since the Liverpool D.M. Only seven Lodges remained: Bury, Blackburn, Birmingham, Halifax, Oldham, Derby and Nottingham, with a total of 81 members. McDermott devotes much of his report to deploring the secession of nine former lodges—more than half the overall strength of the society. As a commentary on the prevailing climate at that time his report makes sad reading.

" Manchester was suspended and ultimately withdrew in 1847 and has been placed before the Association. Their debt to the Association was £29 8s. Liverpool case will be found in the Reports, years 1848-49 and 1851. York and Leicester will be found in Reports 1848-9. Sheffield: previous to the year 1848 no debtor or creditor account was kept by the Corresponding Secretary, neither were there books or other documents whereby the position, financial or otherwise, of the Association could be ascertained. But with the issue of present laws a uniform and clear method of keeping general accounts and the issue of a yearly report was adopted. With this improvement many lodges refused to comply, and on this point Sheffield withdrew, urging that the alterations were unnecessary and injurious, and could not be induced to come back to make the returns required. Wigan: through internal misrule and without notice to general body, this lodge broke up and divided their funds in 1849. An attempt was made to reform in 1850 but the fund was not restored and at the close of 1851 they broke up again owing the Association £2. Rochdale: expenses last year only amounted to £1 5s. 2d., they having been paid 19s. 8d. of the old debt due by Manchester defalcations with a further £3 to receive. Since the close of last year nothing has been heard of this lodge. Bradford: this lodge either through apathy of members or influence of some opposed to Union, are not in compliance. Wolverhampton: this lodge opened under most favourable circumstances with a fund of £30, young and healthy members, an increasing town trade, but were neglectful to leave the affairs in the hands of a few members and the Corresponding Secretary could not induce them to bank their funds in accordance with rules. Some fraud has now taken place but the members have only themselves to blame. Selfishness, jealousy, dishonesty and internal misrule are the primary causes of the failures. However unjustifiable the conduct of those who object to the present method of keeping accounts, now that it is adopted and its superiority over the old admitted, it is probable those lodges will return. It must be acknowledged that the establishing of the Reserve Fund would materially tend to prevent a recurrence of those evils alike injurious to individuals and the entire trade."

On the evidence of Raymond Postgate, there was a further decline in the fortunes of the plumbers over the years up to 1860, in common with most of the building trade unions. This was the period of Richard Harnott, general secretary of the Stonemasons from 1847 until his death in 1872, under whose administration " the old system of Trade Union organisation was developed as far as it possibly could be without a radical change." At that time unions were still regarded, says Postgate, " as simply a fraternal alliance of Lodges. The Lodge was the unit, the real living body; the Central Committee, and its secretary, a mere connecting link whose functions were theoretically little more than those of a post-office. The making of such a body into an efficient industrial weapon, even according to the ideas of 1850, was a

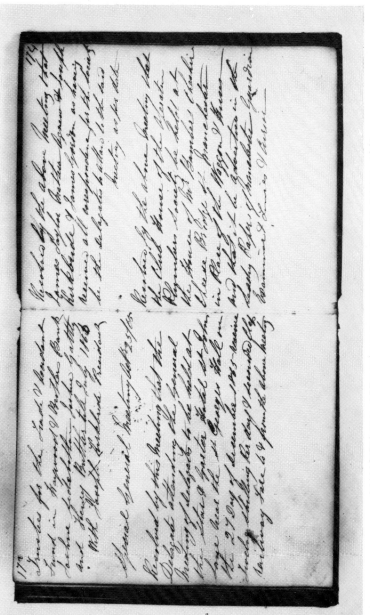

MANCHESTER OPERATIVE PLUMBERS MINUTE BOOK, 1865

Minutes of Special General Meeting, 25th October, at which delegates were appointed to attend the inaugural meeting of the national association, December 1865

UNITED OPERATIVE PLUMBERS ASSOCIATION—DELEGATE MEETING, DUBLIN, 1870
George May (C.S.) is seated sixth from left : on his left is *Charles Cayless* (G.M.P.)

serious task." Harnott's policy was directed towards the limiting of the power of lodges, the centralisation of authority and finance, and the laying of foundations for a strong, national society. In this, he set an example which other unions were soon to follow.

A crisis in the history of the building unions, and a landmark in their development, arose in 1859. Little or no progress had been made since the calamitous strike of 1846 towards the building workers' objective of a nine-hour day. After sporadic but fruitless agitation here and there, a permanent conference of building trade union delegates was convened in 1858 with the object of remaining in being until the nine-hour day was a reality. The conference and its campaigns were under the leadership of George Potter, a carpenter, who put his trust initially in petitions to the employers and propaganda among the operatives rather than in strikes or the threat of strikes. He succeeded in achieving two things: he stirred the interest and imagination of the building workers and incensed the London master builders (who needed scant provocation to put them in an ill humour). The *Illustrated Times* of 6th August, 1859, asked peevishly: " How on earth can a body of uneducated labourers add to the truth on any subject by gathering together into a mob? "

In spite of Potter's pacific approaches, the master builders were only too ready for a fight. The ensuing conflict was precipitated by one of the largest building firms in London, Trollope's of Pimlico (later to become Trollope and Colls), who dismissed from their employment the journeyman mason heading a delegation which presented a petition. London Mason's lodges immediately withdrew their members from Trollope's contract in Knightsbridge and all remaining employees came out, on the recommendation of the building workers' conference, on 21st July, 1859. As on earlier occasions, the response of the master builders was a general lock-out. Within a fortnight, 24,000 men were idle.

Yet another form of the " document " was drawn up by the Central Master Builders' Association. It read: " I declare that *I am not now,* nor will I during the continuance of my engagement with you, become a *member of or support any society* which directly or indirectly interferes with the arrange-

C

ments of this or any other Establishment *or the hours or terms of labour,* and that I recognise the right of Employers and Employed individually *to make any trade engagements on which they may choose to agree."*

This document, when presented to the building operatives, failed to have the effect anticipated by the employers. There was, on this occasion, no scramble to return to the shops: in fact, the labour situation deteriorated to the extent that the masters could hardly secure any labourers. They were also disconcerted by critical Press comment; Raymond Postgate points out that " the attitude of the governing class of England as a whole had undergone a change, and they were no longer prepared to approve entirely of the ' knock-out ' policy of the master builders."

Weakening under the pressure of public opinion, the masters withdrew their written document and demanded a verbal declaration on similar lines. This half-hearted retreat merely underlined the moral superiority of the operatives. The builders' conference instructed the men to abandon the nine-hour claim and concentrate their efforts on persuading the employers to withdraw the document completely. Unfortunately, the perversity of the employers—embarrassed by their recent *faux pas*—once again asserted itself and they refused to make peace. The struggle dragged on into the winter.

For the first time in British trade union history, however, solidarity amongst the workers and sympathy for the building operatives in London was expressed in startling financial terms. Contributions to the dispute fund poured in from societies large and small. The Amalgamated Society of Engineers (forerunner of the A.E.U.) created a sensation by donating a thousand pounds a week for three weeks. The moral effect alone of this gesture on the building workers was incalculable. After a last-ditch exhibition of stubbornness and ill-temper the employers finally threw in their hand, announcing the general withdrawal of the " document " on 7th February, 1860.

Once again, we leave the last word to Raymond Postgate. " The impression which the struggle had made on the mind of every worker was deep. It was only a half-victory, but it had shown to the non-unionists how a very powerful, wealthy and obstinate association of employers could be defied. It had also shown to the unionists how ineffective their own organisations were. . . . When they were finally locked-out they were only saved from disaster because they were able to bring into the fight the whole trade union resources of England and Scotland. Thus we find, as a result of the lock-out, both a great influx of members into existing unions, and a movement towards the reconstruction of existing societies upon a new basis. . . . Plasterers, Painters, Carpenters and Joiners and Plumbers formed new organisations altogether. A complete change of policy, ideas and personnel came over the whole of the British trade union movement after the great lock-out of 1860."

Thus the year 1860 was a turning point in the affairs of organised labour. Gone were the days when small, local craft societies with meagre memberships and primitive rules could function in isolation from their fellow workers in other parts of the country. The time was ripe for change and development. The strength of unity had been demonstrated and the weaknesses of existing combinations exposed. The plumbers of Great Britain were among those who seized the opportunity of closing their ranks.

CHAPTER II

BIRTH OF THE
NATIONAL ORGANISATION

EXACTLY how the seeds were sown, and by whom, we cannot determine. Raymond Postgate states that in 1865 the Manchester Plumbers' Society " entered into negotiations with the local Liverpool Society, and between them they agreed upon the basis for a National Plumbers' Society. The Secretary of the Liverpool Society, J. H. Dobb, then called a conference in Liverpool, to which these rules were submitted."

Beyond this brief and comparatively uninformative report must surely lie a story of imagination, enthusiasm and painstaking preparation. Unfortunately the details are lost in obscurity. Our first printed records of the national association start abruptly in the middle of the report for the December quarter, 1866—nearly twelve months after the critical conference which finally brought the plumbers of the United Kingdom into unity. For earlier detail we have only one or two surviving documents to which we can refer. Possibly the most important of these, from an historical point of view, is the first report issued by J. H. Dobb, in his own handwriting, which has been in the possession of Preston Lodge until it was lent to us for scrutiny in the preparation of this history. This report, apparently issued in April 1866, is valuable not only for the Secretary's remarks but also for the details it contains of Lodges then functioning, with names and addresses of secretaries and other officers and information on Lodge meeting places. There is also a complete register of members, totalling 892. The text of Bro. Dobb's remarks is reproduced as Appendix 2.

The title page of the original Rule Book reveals that the conference at which the " United Operative Plumbers' Association of Great Britain and Ireland " was inaugurated, held in the Star and Garter Hotel, St. John's Lane, Liverpool, from 27th-30th December, 1865, was attended by delegates from thirteen towns: Liverpool, Manchester, Edinburgh, Glasgow, Dublin, Bradford, Birmingham, Chester, Dundee, Lancaster, Preston, Blackburn and Leicester. These Lodges were to form the nucleus of the new organisation, soon to be joined by others at Rochdale, Birkenhead, Bury, Belfast, Greenock, Halifax, Leeds, Newcastle, Oldham, Wakefield, Aberdeen, Inverness, Kendal, Nottingham, Perth, Stirling and York.

The object of the Association, set out in Rule 1, was " the protection and advancement of the trade, and to assist its members when out of employment, or in sickness caused through accident; or in case of death, a sum of money to be allowed for the decent interment of its members."

Contributions were fixed at 3d. a week, and it is worth noting that in the beginning, as now, it was necessary for a member to pay twelve months' contributions before he became entitled to full benefit. The sum allowed for unemployment benefit was 5s. a week for a maximum of 12 weeks in a year; members disabled by accident could claim 10s. a week for three months, 8s. a week for the next three months, 5s. a week for the following six months and 4s. a week thereafter. Funeral benefit was £10 for the next of kin where a member died as a result of an accident, or £5 when death occurred from natural causes. There were half-benefits for members with more than six but less than twelve months' membership.

The conduct of the Association's business was entrusted to a General Managing Committee — the forerunner of the modern Executive Council. General Law 7 declared that " their duties shall be to the association as a lodge committee is to a lodge. . . ." The G.M.C. consisted of five members who, together with a General Managing President (G.M.P.), Vice-President (G.M.V.P.) and Corresponding Secretary (C.S.) were elected at each successive Delegate Meeting.

The Association's original officers, elected at the 1865 conference, were as follows: —

G.M.P.	Matthew Agnew (Manchester)
G.M.V.P.	Edward Prime (Birmingham)
G.M.C.	Charles Cayless (Leicester)
	John H. Crighton (Dundee)
	William Gallie (Glasgow)
	Leonard Horner (Bradford)
	William Hilton (Preston)
C.S.	Joseph H. Dobb (Liverpool)

It was written into the original rules that a Delegate Meeting should be held annually. Lodges with more than 15 and less than 50 members could send one delegate; Lodges with 50 or less than 100 members were entitled to two delegates, and Lodges with more than 100 members could send three delegates. The final business of the Annual Delegate Meeting was to be the election of officers for the ensuing year.

The rule book was divided into two sections—Rules, which were confined to Lodge administration, contributions and benefits, and duties of members; and General Laws, which covered the management of the national association and duties of its officers, etc.

General Law 6 in the first rule book set out in detail the duties of the Corresponding Secretary. He had to keep a register of all the members of the union and send an annual return to every Lodge, giving details of full members, half members, new members, members in arrears, and circulate the minutes of the A.D.M. (which he took himself). He was responsible for notifying Lodges each quarter of their financial position and the amounts due to the national body by way of "equalization." This was a method by which the main benefits and expenses of the society were borne proportionately by the Lodges according to the number of members.

The C.S. was also required to keep accounts of all expenditure incurred in the discharge of his duties (i.e., the society's working expenses, including such items as printing, postage, stationery and so on). He was responsible for arranging all the business connected with the Delegate Meeting, for conducting day-to-day correspondence and keeping the Union's records.

If the C.S. failed to send quarterly returns to Lodges, or sent them too late for the quarterly meeting, there was provision in the General Law for fines of 5s. or 2s. 6d. respectively.

It will be obvious that the position of Corresponding Secretary in 1865 was not exactly a nominal one. According to Raymond Postgate, the salary payable to J. H. Dobb was 1½d. per member per quarter, advanced to him by the four principal Lodges—Liverpool, Manchester, Glasgow and

Edinburgh. From an examination of the few financial records of that time it appears that Bro. Dobb would have received little more than £20 in a full year.

We note with interest, however, that after a century of progress and change the responsibilities of the Union's General Secretary today still include most of the items contained in the original General Law in relation to the business, accounts and correspondence of the national body. Fortunately we now have a full-time clerical staff to ease the burden on the Union's chief administrator.

One feature of those early years, which has long since disappeared from our organisation, was the practice of forming a queue for wage increases. At that time, of course, there was no standard rate of wages for craftsmen. Negotiations took place locally in districts, towns and even villages; a multiplicity of rates existed throughout the country. Agreements reached between Lodges and local employers were embodied in the Lodge Bye-laws, which were sent to the G.M.C. for approval. Any infringement of the bye-laws by an employer gave the Lodge the automatic right to withdraw labour if they wished to do so. On the other hand, however, if a Lodge wanted to press for improvements in wages, reductions in hours, or " any other matter for the welfare of its members, not specified in their recognised bye-laws," the first obligation under General Law 13 was to submit a case to the G.M.C., " stating all particulars of their intentions and requirements, the number of Plumbers not in the lodge, and the grounds upon which they expect to gain their object. . . ." The law required at least two months' notice to be given.

Simple approval of the G.M.C. was not enough. When they had decided in favour of the Lodge's application, it had to be submitted to " the whole of the lodges for their approval or otherwise, by taking the votes (for and against the application) of each lodge, the majority of votes to decide. . . ."

If the approval of the G.M.C. was not forthcoming, the Lodge could itself appeal by the same procedure, on the understanding that if the result of the Lodge vote was unfavourable " then the case, as far as the association is concerned, is at an end. . . ." In this eventuality, the law magnanimously declared that the Lodge could go ahead with the application—at its own expense.

Similarly, a careful formula was prescribed for serving strike notices on unyielding employers and for the subsequent behaviour of Lodge officers and members involved. "... All moral means must be used to bring about an arrangement, and no act of violence, threat, intimidation, or abusive language will be countenanced by the association towards employers or non-society men during a strike. . . ."

At the end of the first twelve months, the Union had a total strength of just over 1,500 members in 31 Lodges. In June 1867 the first Annual Delegate Meeting was held at the " Cheshire Cheese " in Bridge Street, Manchester, and was attended by 37 delegates including members of the G.M.C. Only eight Lodges were not represented. For the first two days, however, the conference was repeatedly adjourned to allow the auditors to complete their scrutiny of the Association's accounts. Their delay was attributed to " the irregular manner in which the quarterly reports are sent . . ." (by Lodges).

A number of minor amendments to the rules and general laws were made, but a more significant alteration was proposed by Manchester Lodge, the " parent of the Association." There was a good deal of wisdom in their suggestion that the society's benefits should continue to be limited to those already outlined in the objects of the society, and " without appealing to the members of this Association to provide for their Widows." This was clearly intended to ensure that the society's function of trade protection and advancement should not be hamstrung by excessive financial burdens arising from the discharge of its second function of a friendly society.

One other resolution of the first D.M. is worth mentioning from an historical point of view. The meeting agreed " that it is not in accordance with the principles of this Association that any Lodge take part as a body in any political demonstration."

At the conclusion of the 1867 Delegate Meeting, Matthew Agnew was re-elected President and Joseph H. Dobb continued as C.S., while William Forster of Dublin became the Association's Vice-President. Newcastle and Edinburgh secured their first representation on the G.M.C. in the persons of Alexander Youngson and John Ainslie respectively.

In the introductory remarks to the quarterly report for June 1867, Dobb reveals that several applications for permission to seek wage increases were awaiting the consideration of the G.M.C. This was a sign of the general prosperity then prevailing. In spite of the fact that strikes still took place, there was a strong tendency during his period on the part of employers to placate the organised workers and to attempt to blunt their militarism by means of propaganda and education. Raymond Postgate says: " Temperance, hard work and self-improvement with a view to rising from the ranks were recommended as the sole means of advancement to the working class. Trade unions were dismissed briefly as nearly uselsss, with a word of praise, if at all, for their friendly benefits. This educational war of the employers . . . had a deep effect upon the minds of the Victorian workers."

The rising tide of national prosperity, however, was not reflected in the workers' wage packets. In the summer of 1867, Edinburgh plumbers were receiving 5½d. an hour and working 51½ hours a week: while in Leicester the plumber's rate was 25s. for a 58½-hour week—" about 5s. per week less than other trades in the building line," as J. H. Dobb commented. But this was not the worst. In the October report, members in Stirling were stated to be seeking an advance of 2s. a week as they felt " they were the lowest paid of any in the plumbing trade." Their rate was 22s. a week.

In the same year, a protracted dispute occurred in Preston. Beginning in July, it remained unresolved until the following March. Nor was the conclusion a satisfactory one: after visits to the employers by members of the G.M.C. and other officers, agreement was eventually reached that the Preston members should return to work on the old terms " providing the employers did not attempt to force them to leave their Lodge." Unity in the young association was strained to the limit. Many Lodges deeply resented the drain on their funds caused by such a fruitless nine-month dispute in a single town, which had brought no apparent benefit either to the members involved or to the Union in general.

The year 1868 was marked by two particular events in the

affairs of the U.O.P.A. In June, the second Delegate Meeting was held in Glasgow; one of the more important decisions was that subsequent Delegate Meetings would be held each alternate year instead of annually. A rather acrimonious dispute occurred between the Manchester delegates and the G.M.C. over the legality of the humiliating strike at Preston. In spite of attempts by delegates from Glasgow and Newcastle to mollify Manchester, the latter's protest was pressed to a vote; the D.M. upheld the G.M.C. and declared the Preston strike to be legal. This clash, however, was the first indication that Manchester was not at all happy with the trend towards centralisation of finance, and serious repercussions were to follow a few years later. The proceedings ended by agreeing that the salary of the C.S. should be increased to 7d. per member per year.

Later in the year, in spite of the fact that he had been re-elected at the D.M., Joseph Dobb resigned as C.S. His place was taken by George May, a Liverpool member who had first appeared in the records as a delegate to the 1868 D.M. At the time he made his first report on 1st October, 1868, the Union had 1,664 members spread over 36 Lodges. Thus, after three years, progress had not been impressive, although it is worth noting that the beginning of 1869 saw the entry into the Union of the first Lodge in the south of England—Bristol, with 19 members.

The enemy, even in those distant days, was one with which we ourselves are only too familiar: apathy. George May appealed to the members in July 1869 for " *a little more interest in the working of the Association, that instead of it being one or two only in each Lodge who seem to care how it is worked,* we may have a fair percentage of the 1,600, who will show by acts that they have the welfare of the Association in their minds, and by it prove without a doubt, that where ' Unity ' is employed, ' Strength ' must follow, so that we can take up our motto without fear that we are ' United to support, but not combined to injure '." Lodges were continually being reprimanded for carelessness in financial matters.

Towards the end of 1869, voting figures were published on a recommendation made by the G.M.C. and put before all

Lodges that the accounts of Lodges, *vis-a-vis* the national body, should be settled each quarter. From a total membership of 1,558, it is recorded that 919 votes were cast in favour of quarterly settlement and 201 against. These figures may seem irrelevant; but in the light of subsequent events, which shook the young Association to its core, their importance will become apparent. Of the 201 votes against the G.M.C. recommendation, 200 were recorded by Manchester Lodge.

In the same report, George May intimated the G.M.C.'s intention " to enforce quarterly payments, and request, immediately on the issue of returns, each Lodge will make their amounts of equalisation payable to Mr. John Fairclough " (the Union's Treasurer).

The recommendation was finally embodied in the rules at the 1870 Delegate Meeting in Dublin. Returns were to be made by all Lodges to the C.S. on specified dates, under penalty of moderately severe fines for non-compliance within seven days of the deadlines. Lodges were allowed 28 days after their quarterly meetings in which to remit the amount of equalisation due from them. If Lodge funds were insufficient to meet the liabilities to the U.O.P.A., they were to be made up by levies.

This timid step towards the enforcement of centralisation was not at all popular. It must be remembered, of course, that the national body was only five years old and many Lodges bitterly resented any encroachments on their independence and autonomy, particularly where money was concerned. The September quarterly report contained another rather pompous appeal from the G.M.C. " To those who have not paid, we claim that a levy be made at once to meet their debt, in accordance with the alteration made at the D.M. . . . For really it is a disgrace that we, the most independent class in the Building Trade, should be so backward in paying our share in the expenses incurred."

Clearly, 1870 was a black year. Trade was slack and members drifted away for various reasons—one of which was admitted to be " because they could not see their Lodges accumulating any funds."

Two other important decisions, which were to result in

domestic conflict, were passed at the 1870 Delegate Meeting. By a narrow voting margin the minimum rate of contributions was raised to 4d. a week, and payment of out-of-work benefit was limited to 48 days instead of 72 days. On the next morning, the Manchester delegate, supported by Bradford, moved a proposal demanding that a Lodge vote be taken on these two decisions before they became effective. These same two delegates had unsuccessfully opposed the increase of 1d. a week in the minimum contribution, but this time they carried the day. The issues were referred to the Lodges.

The result of the Lodge vote was an endorsement of the original decisions of the D.M. on these two issues. Unfortunately for the Association, so far as Manchester was concerned this was not the end of the affair. Once again they returned a " block vote " of 200 on each question—but this time the G.M.C. were having none of it. In the first quarterly report for 1871 the relevant correspondence between George May and the secretary of Manchester Lodge, James Gordon, is published in full. " It will be remembered," says May, " that the delegates assembled at Dublin in June last submitted to the Association two very important questions for their decision, and it was decided that ' all secretaries should send the number of the members present at the meetings when these questions were put.' Every Lodge that *did* vote carried out this rule, with the exception of Manchester, which claimed on each question 200 votes."

After a long and bitter exchange of letters, the G.M.C. eventually decided that Manchester's vote should be omitted from the final returns, " being satisfied that the number of 200 sent as having voted on the above, was not present at the meeting." Manchester subsequently refused to see a deputation from the G.M.C., repudiated their equalisation liabilities for the July quarter, and tendered their resignation from the society. In his final comment at the end of the correspondence, George May remarks: " This is the treatment we have received from the ' parent ' of the Association— we find ourselves deserted by our ' heartless parent '; but not without hope. ' He ' may yet repent . . . and at some time, not far distant, we may again renew our acquaintance with Manchester."

Some of the troubles of this period can undoubtedly be attributed to the failure of the plumbers to follow the example of other unions and establish their society on firm " amalgamated " foundations with power held securely at the top. The United Society of Operative Plumbers was still little more than a loose federation of local societies, each with their own ideas, prejudices and weaknesses. Moreover, from the remarks made by George May that plumbers were " the most independent class in the Building Trade " it can be inferred that what might be construed as the simple pride of craftsmen was, in fact, something a little closer to snobbery. This inference is substantiated by the fact that no attempt was made to widen the range of entry to the society: indeed, the rules were quite positive that membership should be open only to those " competent to earn their livelihood as Plumbers." This deep-rooted conservatism cannot be wholly condemned, since it was symptomatic of the social and moral climate in general, and of the attitude of the artisan class in particular, over the years that had gone before. Nevertheless, it was a tendency that persisted throughout the Union's early history and obviously had a retarding effect upon its potential membership and industrial development.

That the secession of Manchester in 1870 was a serious blow to the national society is undeniable: but it did not result, as it might well have done, in disintegration. The G.M.C. received assurances of support from several Lodges and the society's business continued as before.

Fortunately, there were other factors which helped to restore society's equilibrium. The early 1870s saw a trade recovery and renewed industrial prosperity. Trade unionists in general were encouraged by the success of the annual Trades Union Congress which had first assembled in 1868— at Manchester. The " nine-hour movement " was resuscitated, and there was revived opposition to trade unionism in certain Parliamentary legislation, notably the Criminal Law Amendment Act, which had the effect of closing the ranks of trade unionists and strengthening their organisations. This particular Act made all picketing illegal; it was regarded by all unions, including our own, as a threat to organised workers throughout the country. " If ever there was a time when

' unity ' was necessary it is the present," said George May in the last report of 1871, " for only by unity can the obnoxious Criminal Law Amendment Act be repealed, the many disadvantages of which have been plainly shown since it became law, and calls for a united effort to rid us of the danger we are placed in so long as it remains law."

Also in 1871 came the first Trade Union Act, under which all trade unions could legally register and so protect their funds from internal embezzlement. As Francis Williams remarks in *Magnificent Journey*: " With the one hand combinations of workers were given the right to exist. With the other the means to make their existence effective in terms of the industrial struggle was taken away."

For the U.O.P.A., 1872 opened with bright hopes for the future, the state of trade being truly encouraging. . . ." Leicester Lodge was among the first to apply for permission to seek improvements in wages and conditions by asking the employers " to reduce the hours of labour from $58\frac{1}{2}$ to 51 hours per week and that the rates of wages be 6d., $6\frac{1}{4}$d. and $6\frac{1}{2}$d. per hour, instead of 25s., 26s. and 27s. per week." Manchester Lodge, still " beyond the pale," had issued a lengthy pamphlet about their reasons for secession and were being accused by the G.M.C. of attempting " to sow discord amongst our members by . . . a misrepresentation of the circumstances." It is clear that any possibility of a reconciliation seemed, at that time, very remote indeed; although a few of the members in Manchester had, in fact, remained with the U.O.P.A. who appointed a relieving officer in the town to look after their interests.

During the second quarter of 1872, strikes took place in Oldham, Dundee and Kendal by the members, who had received G.M.C. authority to " endeavour to advance the interests of our Trade." In the light of modern costs it is interesting to note that the total expenses involved in the three disputes were £17 9s., £11 2s. and £1 respectively. In each case the strike was successful and a wage increase of $\frac{1}{2}$d. an hour was secured. The G.M.C. were obviously beginning to recognise the serious difficulties created by the stipulation of the Rule that only one Lodge at a time could make application for advances: two of the larger Lodges,

Glasgow and Dublin, were reported as having " successfully
obtained the terms of their applications on their own responsibility . . . not being prepared to take their turn according
to rule. In each of these cases our conduct has been found
fault with, but we have simply carried out the rules that
guide us, and upon which we feel bound to act; at the same
time, we consider that considerable alterations are required
to make the rule ' for the advancement of our Trade ' work
with more advantage."

In spite of further successes in various districts " without
any struggle," a second blow struck the U.O.P.A. in 1872
by the secession of Glasgow. " Glasgow leaves to start business for themselves," says the report, " and has not been
backward in endeavouring to sow discord amongst the Scotch
lodges by asserting that the funds of the association are
' eaten up by English lodges,' and that our rules are defective
and the benefits difficult to obtain; they had not the moral
courage to state these to us, but they take two very sly
methods to spread these untruths (for a perusal of our returns
will at once refute the assertions). In the Scotch papers we
find a report of one of their meetings informing Scotland that
they have new rules prepared for forming a Scotch Association. . . . We exhort Lodge secretaries to use every legitimate
means to induce any Glasgow members who are at present
paying into their lodges, or who are working in their respective towns, to be at once transferred, and not to throw away
such substantial benefits as those offered by our Association."

The year ended on a slightly more optimistic note with the
announcement of the opening of a new Lodge in Manchester,
with a nucleus of twelve members. For the first time, however, there is reference to a practice that has bedevilled trade
unionism—and particularly the craft unions—from its early
days. " One of the employers at Bradford has been taking
advantage of the journeymen in his employ by giving to
unskilled labourers some portion of his work, which, of course,
was resisted by our members; we are sorry to say, not successfully, for unprincipled men have been found, and are now
filling the places of those formerly employed." A familiar
situation from the long-forgotten past!

One of the alterations to rule made at the 1870 Dublin

D.M. was to increase again the interval between Delegate Meetings. It will be remembered that the D.M. was originally an annual event; then it became biennial, and from 1870 it was to be held every third year. The main reason was obviously shortage of finance: the funds of the Association in the early 1870s were so low that the G.M.C. could meet only once a year (at Preston in 1871 and Dundee in 1872) and the Association's business was left almost entirely in the hands of George May, part-time Corresponding Secretary. There was no income other than contributions. These had been raised by 1d. a week in 1870; any subsequent financial benefit, however, had largely been offset by the disastrous loss of Manchester and Glasgow—two of the largest of the original Lodges.

The hard facts of the situation were recognised, to some extent, by the 34 delegates who met in Edinburgh for the fourth D.M. in June 1873. Their remedies, however, were too feeble and timid to provide effective solutions to the problems of dwindling finances. In the first place, the G.M.C. took the initiative in proposing that the national association be relieved of all responsibility for payment of out-of-work benefit. " The intention," they declared, " is simply to allow each lodge to pay such sum, as out-of-work pay, as they may deem just, but that it be not included in the equalisation." At the D.M., the G.M.C.'s proposal was endorsed by 22 votes to 11, and the minimum rate of contribution was increased from 4d. to 6d.

The effects of these two decisions were largely negated by the introduction of Sickness Benefit in the wider definition— it had previously been paid only in cases resulting from industrial accidents—and to provide benefit at the rate of 10s. a week for three months, 6s. a week for the second three months and 4s. a week thereafter. This new benefit became effective from June 1874.

One minor amendment to rule, demanding that a financial statement be sent to the C.S. annually by all lodges, produced a tie in the voting: 17 for and 17 against. The Chairman (Daniel Luke, of Stirling) used his casting vote in favour of the proposition—which emanated from Edinburgh.

There was an unsuccessful attempt to increase strike pay

Fellow Member,

The Present report is submitted to your notice as the first report issued by the Association. It having only been in existence since December last, and in consequence, we have not got into proper working order; so that allowances must be made for any imperfection that may appear; trusting that as we proceed we may gain experience and improve, and that the Association may prove both useful and beneficial to all connected with it; and be the means of putting an end to disputes, and creating a better feeling between both employers and employees. We have this quarter opened two additional Lodges one at Rochdale, and one at Bolton, and I am happy to state that we have 3 more applications for opening Lodges, one at Newcastle on Tyne at Leeds and Stirling. I may inform you that it is at present under consideration at Dundee and Lancaster to ask for an advance on their present rate of wages, as they only receive 21/ per week; should there happen to be a dispute, (which I do not think probable from the information I have received) I will send to each Lodge an account of the same, when all that choose can send, aid, if required by them. Earnestly hoping that every member will use his influence and endeavour as far as lays in their power to strengthen the union, members knowing of any Lodges not in connection will oblige by giving the address so that they may be communicated with; with the view to their joining the Association. With best wishes to all allow me to remain

Yours Respectfully

J H Dobb

8 Marquis Street,
Liverpool

Joseph H. Dobb's first report to the members of the United Operative
Plumbers' Association, April, 1866

GLASGOW EXECUTIVE COUNCIL 1895

George B. Cherry (G.S.) is second from left in the front row, and on the extreme right is *E. E. Burns*

from 12s. to 15s. a week, but the advice given by the G.M.C. on the necessity to alter the strike rule was taken to heart and authority was given to the G.M.C. to permit more than one application to go forward at the same time. This, at least, was a step in the right direction so far as principles were concerned, but the wisdom of its acceptance in the light of the association's financial position is difficult to justify.

Quarterly reports for 1874 show that the attention of the G.M.C. was increasingly occupied by the financial problems that beset the Association. They were legion. Lodge after Lodge earned the censure of the auditors for the " gross carelessness " responsible for errors in the returns and the " unbusinesslike way " in which payments were transmitted and recorded. Above all, however, repeated emphasis was laid on the need for Lodges to provide their own funds to cover the immediate expense of strikes; in fact, the G.M.C. demanded that any Lodge seeking improvements in wages and conditions should first furnish a statement of the exact financial position of the Lodge, as it was found that " some Lodges make application and even enter upon a strike without making the slightest preparation for the struggle beforehand. . . . The real principle of our system of equalisation is to divide the expenses equally after it has been incurred, and not to provide money to meet the expenses incurred by Lodges during the quarter." The G.M.C. considered that at least a fortnight's strike pay should be available in advance of a dispute.

During the first three months of operation the new Sickness Benefit was found to have cost about 7d. per member. Thus the increase of 2d. a week in contributions appeared to be adequate, but the G.M.C. warned Lodge officers " to be particular in dispensing (sick benefit), to be careful that none but legitimate claims are paid, and to introduce a system of visiting suitable to the circumstances."

The annual meeting of the G.M.C. at Liverpool in June 1875 was mainly spent on financial business, but the Committee did record their appreciation of the opening of a new Lodge in Glasgow by members from Edinburgh, who " were entitled to great praise for the successful way in which they had carried out the promise made by their delegate at the last D.M." Prospects of healing the breach in Glasgow

D

seemed encouraging; the G.M.C. were discussing the bye-laws of the new Lodge "and the question of their jointly acting with the old Lodge in Glasgow in seeking new privileges or protecting existing ones." But trouble—never far away—was now brewing in another quarter. A resolution passed at a meeting of Liverpool Lodge called attention to what were considered the "enormous" expenses of management. The G.M.C. "played it cool" and offered to explain any item "that may seem to be not in accordance with law. . . ." By the end of the year, however, the cloud had burst with a thunderclap with Liverpool demanding the resignation of the entire G.M.C., who in turn opened fire on their accusers with all guns and appointed one auditor each from Dublin, Edinburgh and Nottingham "to audit the accounts for the present year . . . and to ascertain the correctness, or otherwise, of the charges financial made by Liverpool against the Auditors' balance sheets for past years and report to the D.M., leaving it to the discretion of delegates to order an audit by a public accountant if considered advisable." So ended the first decade of the United Operative Plumbers' Assocation—"full of sound and fury."

Despite the internal squabbles, financial strictures and ponderous government, however, the progress made in the Association's first ten years was by no means insubstantial. From the nucleus of a dozen small Lodges the Association had extended its influence throughout the land until at the end of 1875 it could claim a membership of nearly 2,000 spread over 50 Lodges. The original rules had been clarified, enlarged and adapted in the light of experience. The Association had survived the defection of its "heartless parent"—Manchester—in 1870 and the breakaway of Glasgow two years later. Most important, however, it had demonstrated the truth of the maxim "unity is strength" by co-ordinating, however clumsily at the beginning, the efforts of plumbers throughout the kingdom to "maintain and improve the conditions of their working lives."

CHAPTER III

GEORGE CHERRY LEADS THE PLUMBERS

THE year 1876 saw the U.O.P.A. hold its fifth Delegate Meeting in Nottingham. For several reasons, it was a critical meeting in the Union's development.

Early in the proceedings, George May submitted his resignation as Corresponding Secretary after eight years in office; his place was taken by William J. Barnett of Nottingham, who was elected by a narrow majority over an Edinburgh opponent—J. Henderson—to become the Association's first full-time Secretary at a salary of £120 a year.

The meeting also agreed to abolish the General Managing Committee and substitute an Executive Committee of eight members. These were to be elected annually by and from the Lodges in the towns selected by the D.M. to be the Union's hadquarters for the three periods of twelve months following the Delegate Meeting. Raymond Postgate describes this peculiar procedure much more clearly, though disapprovingly: " The members started a great game with the Executive Committee, chasing it up and down the country like a football. In 1876 the seat of government was moved to Newcastle; no sooner had the office got settled there than it was sent up to Edinburgh: next year again (1878) it was dragged down to Bolton and next year sent across country to Hull, then it was ordered away to vegetate in Sunderland. . . ."

No doubt this unfortunate experiment was introduced in good faith as an attempt to placate the critics who claimed vociferously, but with little justification, that Lodges in the vicinity of Union headquarters received more favourable attention than those in remote parts of the country. The fact that the proposals were of Scottish origin is also significant. Certain other decisions relating to the administrative structure of the Association were more practical. The E.C. were to meet weekly and were to " provide apartments . . . as a place of meeting for the E.C., and whereat the C.S. may reside, the rent to be equally appointed between the association and the C.S." They were also authorised to demand immediate access to the books of any Lodge for examination,

and were instructed to register the Association to ensure the
future protection of its funds.

George May's services did not go unrecognised. At the
end of the D.M. he was presented with "a very handsome
timepiece," suitably inscribed, by the G.M.P. (George Lymath
of Birmingham) at a meeting in the Lord Nelson Inn, Carlton
Street, Nottingham. Three months later he handed over the
reins to his full-time successor, W. J. Barnett.

Trade was very bad in the early months of 1877, fore-
shadowing the beginning of long years of economic depression.
Nevertheless, the Association made steady progress under its
new arrangements. Membership rose to over 2,300, finances
were strengthened, and many wage applications were successfully pursued. The proposed registration of the Association
under the Trade Union Act, 1871, had to be abandoned; the
E.C. reported that there were so many difficulties, including
a complete alteration of rules, the establishment of a
permanent registered office, and so on, that the decision was
impossible to implement.

One innovation during the year was publicised by the E.C.
This was "the advantageous working of a small separate
fund which has been established in several of our Lodges and
is called a Benevolent Fund, and is raised by members paying
one penny per fortnight, and after contributing six months,
are entitled to have the Lodge contributions paid out of this
fund should they fall sick or be out of employment, and thus
saving a good many from falling in arrears and eventually
being excluded."

A warm welcome was extended "to our old friends from
Manchester," readmitted to the U.O.P.A. as Manchester Local
Lodge after their seven years "in the wilderness." In October
1877, the death was reported of the original Corresponding
Secretary, Joseph Dobb of Liverpool.

Nottingham Lodge, were commended on having successfully
negotiated a rate of 9½d. an hour, effective from April 1878,
which made them "the best-paid branch in the Association."

At the same time, serious efforts were being made to organise
non-unionists. "You will no doubt observe in the C.S.
expenses an item for circulars to non-society men," wrote W.
J. Barnett. "These circulars . . . will be distributed to each

Lodge, to be given to any man who does not belong to us; and in giving them, you can say, ' Here mate, read this some time when you have a few minutes to spare, and tell us what you think about it '; and we hope it may be the means of bringing many sheep into our fold. . . ."

There was certainly justification for the claim made in a later report that 1877 was the most successful year since the Association's foundation. Membership had risen to nearly 2,800—a gain of 500 in the year. This was remarkable progress in those days. A total of £1,400 was paid out in benefits alone. Rising fortunes were not confined to the U.O.P.A., however; all building unions made substantial advances during this period. It must have given cause for jubilation among working men and their union leaders, who can be forgiven for imagining that Utopia was just around the corner. They were shortly to be disillusioned.

In modern times we regard the national economy with much less fatalism than did our Victorian forefathers. " Booms " and " slumps " are considered to be the result of inefficient planning rather than acts of God. In Victorian Britain however, they still occurred with monotonous though apparently unpredictable regularity and little or no action was taken at national level to eradicate the causes of trade depressions, which brought in their train so much untold misery and hardship to working men and women. 1878 saw the onset of such another depression which swept through all industries over the whole country.

Membership of the U.O.P.A., after reaching a peak of 2,843 early in the year, began to decline. Reports of efforts to improve wages and hours of work are supplanted by accounts from all quarters of resistance to wage reductions. Two major disputes at Edinburgh and Nottingham, were expensive failures. In Nottingham, the fiasco was attributed to " the large number of strangers every day pouring into the town, through the employers issuing advertisements, pamphlets and circulars throughout every town in the kingdom—in fact, resorting to every oppressive and unwarrantable means to not only keep the men out, but were actually the means of hindering the men getting work elsewhere, and the only terms they can obtain work at is a halfpenny reduction of wage and an

entire new code of bye-laws drawn up by the employers
(which entirely annihilates their own), also they must sign a
six-months agreement, and each man must send a letter to
the masters' secretary asking for work and agreeing to have
nothing whatever to do with the Plumbers' Association. On
these and no other terms can they obtain work." " There
never was a time," declared the E.C., "when it was so
necessary for trade unionists to be firmly banded together to
resist the great exertions of combined Capitalists to entirely
crush unionism out of existence; of which the Nottingham
employers are a striking instance."

The outlook was black indeed, and was deepened by the
announcement of the death of another stalwart of the Association: George May, " one who was always ready and willing
to assist for the common good."

Bolton was now Union headquarters, providing the E.C.
for what must have been one of the most unpromising years
in the Association's existence. Membership had already
fallen by about 200 and expenditure was " enormous." Some
idea of the financial losses can be imparted by a comparison
of figures for dispute benefit for the two consecutive periods
of twelve months: in 1877 the total was £416, while in 1878
it reached £2,446—nearly six times as much. These figures
clearly put the wind up the E.C. (as well they might), since
in the last report for 1878 they were suggesting that Lodges
should seriously consider whether it was worth while resisting
the " numerous encroachments upon our wages and working
customs " that were expected to multiply if the depression
continued. The burden of another Delegate Meeting, only
six months distant, according to rule, was felt in the circumstances best avoided, and by a large majority Lodges voted
in favour of postponement. January 1879 saw the resignation
of the C.S., W. J. Barnett, in spite of " every endeavour to
persuade him to retain his position." Obviously he decided
there was no future in moving house every twelve months and
trying simultaneously to nurse the Association through such
turbulent times.

Frequently, adversity seems to produce outstanding
personalities. Possibly the persons become outstanding
because of their approach to the difficulties facing them when

they are called to office. Be that as it may, the dire state of affairs of the U.O.P.A. in 1879 coincided with the appointment of George Baker Cherry as Corresponding Secretary. Cherry was a member of Hull Lodge, which provided the Executive Committee for twelve months from September 1879. He took up his appointment at a time when the Association's efforts were directed not towards improvements in wages and hours, not even towards resisting reductions in wages and worsening of working conditions, but merely to containing the downward movement within limits. This is not to suggest that the Association was cowed or routed by employers' attacks on living standards: on the contrary, where resistance was considered justified the members took firm action. Nevertheless, for financial reasons alone there had to be severe restrictions on the measure of retaliatory action that could be taken. The atmosphere generally, when Cherry took over, must have been one of grim determination.

Raymond Postgate declares that with the appointment of Cherry, the U.O.P.A. gained something in strength and more in reputation. " He was an official of the older type, obstinate and narrow in many ways, his views confined to his craft, but energetic, of enormous force of character, able, unquestionably honest—in short, a man much of the type of Richard Harnott. Cherry gave the society stability and some rudiments of a coherent policy. . . ."

Reductions of a penny an hour were announced by employers in Liverpool and Manchester to take effect early in 1880. The E.C. announced that the reductions would be resisted. A lock-out ensued in Liverpool and Birkenhead, during which the employers offered a novel solution: arbitration. The offer was, however, subject to the operatives' acceptance of a halfpenny reduction. As the E.C. pointed out, " to go to work on the latter clause of the resolution would practically acknowledge the acceptance of $\frac{1}{2}$d. an hour reduction, and then the question for Arbitrators to consider would be not as to the advisability of the proposed reduction of 1d. an hour, but as how much they could conscientiously allow the Artizan to retain of the remaining $\frac{1}{2}$d." The lock-out continued. Every member in employment was to be levied to the extent of 5s. a week for the support of the locked-out Merseysiders. Resistence was eventually justified by the Arbitrator's award of a reduction of ¼d. an hour.

One bright spot in the " cloud that overshadowed " the U.O.P.A. was the establishment of the first U.O.P.A. Lodge in London. George Cherry and the E.C. Vice-President were invited to the opening ceremony of London No. 1 Lodge. No more than eight members constituted the Association's foothold in the Metropolis—but at least it was a start. Within the year other Lodges were inaugurated at Lewisham and Crystal Palace.

The struggles of 1879 left their mark on the Association in more ways than one. There was a welcome diminution in the parochialism that hindered progress towards centralisation of power and co-ordination of efforts in the Lodges. When the postponed Delegate Meeting finally took place in Hull in the summer of 1880, an important step was taken to strengthen the Union's financial foundation by accepting the proposals drawn up by a specially appointed committee for the establishment of a Reserve Fund. Twopence a week was to be set aside from every member's contribution for a period of two years, and a penny a week thereafter; the Fund, to be used only for payment of strike and incapacitation benefits, was to be maintained at a figure of not less than £1,000. Quite obviously, there was general agreement among the delegates, stimulated no doubt by recent bitter experience, that not only " unity " was " strength ": unity was essential, certainly—but it would not feed empty bellies in time of dispute.

The 1880 D.M. also decided that Raymond Postgate's " football "—the Executive Committee—should be booted around the country rather less frequently—every two years. Three years remained the normal interval between Delegate Meetings, but with a proviso that a vote of Lodges should be taken in advance to confirm that the D.M. should take place. George Cherry was unanimously re-elected as the Association's permanent secretary, and Sunderland was chosen as headquarters until 1882.

After the D.M. was over, the E.C. went to great pains to explain to members the advantages to be expected from the decision to establish a Reserve Fund. No doubt it was essential to do so: not all the parochialism had been extirpated at the meeting in Hull. Having set out at length the reasons why the E.C. were "responsible for the contracts, etc., entered into on behalf of the Association," and condemning the earlier rule which had prevented the Association holding any funds at headquarters, the Executive concluded: "To maintain our position amongst trade associations, and to prevent encroachments upon our trade privileges and customs, we must have capital."

As a sidelight on working conditions at the time it is worth mentioning the report from Hanley of a member who claimed three hours' pay (about two shillings) for carrying his tools home from work. His employer discharged him for making "so extravagant a charge," maintaining that the member should carry the tools home in his own time. The distance had been eleven miles.

Efforts continued in 1881 to regain some of the ground lost in Scotland in 1872. Mass meetings of plumbers were organised in Edinburgh, Glasgow, Aberdeen and Dundee. As the September report pointed out, there were "sufficient grounds for using extraordinary means to try to gain some of the non-society men. We are informed there are about 600 plumbers in Glasgow. In June quarter we had 56 members in our branch, and the U.O.P.A. of Scotland had 64 in their branch." These meetings were attended and addressed by officials of other unions and of local Trades Councils. For the first time, in this report, we find the E.C. recommending Lodges "that are not associated with the Trades Councils to join and take their place in fighting for the principal questions affecting the interests of workmen, as in our opinion it is their duty to take their portion of the burden and expenses of the many important questions that are to be brought before the country through the Trades Union Congress Parliamentary Committee."

Efforts were being made all over the country to extend the influence of the Association; a notable addition in the south of England was Oxford Lodge, opened in August 1881 with eleven members.

Despite the quest for expansion and consolidation, there was still a special place in the heart of the Victorian plumber of 1882 for the traditions and ceremonies of the past. During the first week in September the Festival of the Guild Merchant was held in Preston; this event occurred only once in every twenty years. The secretary of the Preston Plumbers' Guild Committee described the event as one that was " each day celebrated by great rejoicings and events of importance. Upon one of these days the tradesmen of the town form in procession, accompanied by bands of music and regalia, showing working specimens of their handicraft upon lorries, in the form of open workshops, the whole forming a novel and pleasing sight." The plumbers of Preston cordially invited " any member of the Association to accompany them on that occasion."

Even in years of depression and distress, it seems, there was always time and money for a big parade and some flag-waving. Further details were given in June 1882: " Our contingent to the general procession will be headed by the splendid band of the " Indefatigable " training ship, and as many employers as choose to avail themselves of the privilege. Also, a two-pole banner with the Plumbers' coat of arms and suitable inscriptions, to be followed by a two-horse lorry having fixed thereon a full-sized model of general plumbing work, baths, w.-closets, lavatories, kitchen range with cylinder and all necessary pipes and taps complete, so arranged that the public could view the entire mechanism. Another two-horse lorry will contain chancel and windows, roofed over with specimens of ecclesiastical and other glazing; also a full-sized fountain, continuously issuing jets of water, the base surmounted with ferns and other plants, room being reserved upon the lorry for man and assistant at work. The members of the Preston lodge to follow, with as many members of the association as will honour us with their presence. All our local members will wear aprons with the Plumbers' arms lithographed in colour, trimmed with silk fringe and ribbon, beautifully got up, and greatly admired, 5s. 3d. each; rosettes, white gloves, 5d. each; and silk hats. Any member of the Association joining us will be expected to wear similar regalias, aprons optional." It must have been a sight for sore eyes.

The Sunderland E.C. ended its reign in 1882 and the

Association moved south to Birmingham. In the final report from Sunderland, reference was made to the growing dissent among certain Lodges with the retention of the rate of 2d. per member per week for the Reserve Fund. In considerable detail, the E.C. argued their case for leaving the figure unaltered; their aim, they declared, was a Reserve Fund of £10,000—enough to pay strike benefit to every member of the U.O.P.A. for about eight weeks. Here is evidence of the determination of the Association's leaders, faced with a residue of local jealousy and antagonism, to put the U.O.P.A. once and for all beyond the reach of bankruptcy. Credit is surely due to them that in a period of mounting depression, to be unrelieved until 1888, they managed to sustain membership and finances at all. Even the Press had a word of praise: the *Newcastle Weekly Chronicle* said: " A point raised in this is as to the amount of reserve fund the Plumbers' Society should have to meet its demands. . . . As the tendency of trade societies is not to accumulate adequate funds, the efforts most to be commended is that which points to an increase of the moneys accumulated for the use of the members when, during disputes and other times of trial, the strain comes. If the history of trade unionism should ever be carefully written . . . I am certain that it will be found that disruption and failure have come in consequence of the members not having made adequate provision during the more favourable times for the rainy day that sooner or later will come. . . ."

At this period, too, the more progressive outlook of the E.C. was epitomised in their decision to contribute £4 10s. to the support of the T.U.C. Parliamentary Committee. " Our only regret is that such a course has not been adopted before," they commented. Further progress was also being made away from the traditional strongholds of trade unionism with the opening of Lodges at Swansea, Southampton, Exeter and Torquay. Lodges also gave their almost unanimous approval to the suggestion that the Union should at last be registered under the Trade Unions Acts of 1871 and 1876. Registration was, in fact, recorded two years later.

The Delegate Meeting at the Old Crown, Edgbaston Street, Birmingham in 1883 promised to be a lively one. It was a six-day affair and for the first time a long address was

delivered by George Cherry as C.S. on what might be termed
" the state of the Union." We now call it the General Secretary's Report. In this, he dealt with membership, organisation and finance since the previous D.M., at the same time
putting forward his own views on many of the more important
propositions before the meeting.

Nottingham and Cardiff were heavily defeated in their
demand for a return to a twelve-month Executive Committee.
The E.C. themselves had proposed four years, but delegates
compromised by making the period three years. In spite of
the expected attempts to freeze the amount of the Reserve
Fund contribution at a penny a week per member, and even
an attempt to abolish the Fund altogether, Cherry's repeated
exhortations to give the U.O.P.A. a firm financial foundation
had clearly left their mark. The rule was left basically
unchanged and the amount fixed at twopence. Arrangements
were also made for the Fund to be in charge of three Trustees,
one each from England, Scotland and Ireland, to be elected
by ballot at the D.M.

The power of the E.C. was increased slightly by an amendment which authorised them " to determine anything of
emergency wherein the Laws and Rules are silent." Yet
another innovation which has since become an established
part of our machinery was a law introduced by Manchester
and Leicester providing for the election of a Standing Orders
Committee, on the first day of a D.M., whose duty would
be " to consider and report to the D.M. any business that
may be submitted to them."

By a narrow majority it was decided that contributions
should remain at 8d. a week. Proposals sponsored by Liverpool for the introduction of out-of-work benefit were rejected.

Although complimenting George Cherry on his " energy,
perseverance and ability " and re-electing him unanimously,
the D.M. decided to leave his salary at £120 per annum.
Perhaps Cherry drew some small satisfaction from the change
in his title—from " Corresponding Secretary " to " General
Secretary " and the permission granted him to employ an
office-boy.

Later in 1883, following a Lodge vote, the Association was
registered under the Trade Union Acts. Members were being

encouraged to take an interest in technical practices and developments by reading an American publication, *The Sanitary Engineer,* available to U.O.P.A. members at 3d. a copy from the beginning of 1884. More positive support was being urged for the T.U.C. Parliamentary Committee, on which the U.O.P.A. was not represented. " The benefits that we have received as a trade and as members of a community," wrote Cherry, " demand that we should support it." If sufficient support from Lodges was forthcoming, it was proposed to take a vote on the amount of the subscription and the suggestion that the U.O.P.A. should be represented at the annual meeting.

Grave concern was expressed about certain schemes of " accident insurance " being operated by certain employers. At that time, the only legal protection for an injured workman was the opportunity, afforded under the Employers' Liability Act, to sue his employer for damages. This possibility in 1884 for a man earning about 30s. a week in full employment (if he could get it) was, to say the least, rather remote. The E.C. made it quite clear that " if any member is being compelled against his will to support those (insurance) companies, we shall allow such member strike pay in resisting compulsory payment to companies that are entirely for employers' benefit."

It was the overwhelming decision of the Association to send a delegate to the 1884 Annual Congress of the T.U.C. in Aberdeen. The representative was John Petrie of Aberdeen Lodge, who successfully moved a resolution in the following terms: " That, in the opinion of this Congress, it is desirable that only thoroughly practical men should hold the position of sanitary inspectors in our large cities or towns." Not only was the resolution passed unanimously, but with the deletion of the last six words in order to make it universally applicable. The Plumbers were beginning to leave their mark in the wider spheres and councils of trade unionism.

But the economic depression continued. " All Lodges seem to be affected," wrote Cherry in December 1884, " but the shipbuilding districts are the most seriously affected . . . and we learn that the condition of some of our members is wretched."

Beneath the individual miseries and hardships, however, members of the U.O.P.A. were growing more conscious of the importance of their craft. So, too, were the public. Thirteen years earlier the Prince of Wales had been a victim of typhoid fever and the event undoubtedly helped to awaken the public conscience to the appalling state of Victorian sanitation. Early in 1885 the Worshipful Company of Plumbers announced the convening of a special conference of metropolitan and provincial plumbers, with an agenda featuring the following subjects: the technical instruction of plumbers; apprenticeship and indenturing; establishment of boards of examiners; the registration of journeymen plumbers; types and quality of plumbing materials; establishment of district councils to supervise standards of plumbing work; and, finally, arrangements to appeal to Parliament " for necessary amendments and extensions of the law relating to plumbers' work."

First reactions of the E.C. were derisory. " We are aware that the Guild may relapse into its Rip Van Winkle sleep if left alone, but we also want to be prepared to combat and oppose any useless irritating measures that they may propose to enforce upon us. . . . The principal theme is the intolerable ignorance of the plumber. We generally find that those who have never learnt the trade are prepared to advise us. Mr. Magnus, at the Guild dinner, finds that plumbers require more scientific training. We are of the opinion that the man who can go at once and remedy the disease has as much scientific and practical knowledge as is necessary; but some people, when they see the plumber, expect him to give them several problems from Euclid and a Latin quotation or two; then, whether he could do his work or not, he would be the man for them."

Although the Association recognised the value of good plumbing and sanitation, they were clearly not prepared to be told by grandma how to suck eggs. They did, however, continue to give vent to their wrath at the practice of appointing sanitary inspectors " from the lists of retired soldiers, policemen, pensioners, or hangers-on of political parties," when such appointments ought to be made " from a class of men whose trade specially qualifies them for the work of sanitary inspector."

Again in 1885 there is evidence of the tendency noted earlier for plumbers to separate themselves, unconsciously perhaps, from the mass movement of working-class trade unionists towards a common unity and economic freedom. In a report in the *Liverpool Courier* of a public meeting at which presentations of incapacitation grants of £100 each were made to two members of Liverpool Lodge, the Liverpool Lodge secretary, Thomas Anderton, is quoted as declaring that some people thought the trade unions " had largely accomplished the objects for which they were formed " and would now begin to languish. " It should be remembered, however, that hitherto they had been fighting for their rights, but the time was now come when they might in justice and wisdom cast their thoughts a little higher and see how they could raise the working classes to some extent into the ranks above them." A laudable object, to be sure, and one which to a large extent we have seen achieved: but against the background of the ten-year depression and the " wretched condition " of many U.O.P.A. members, it does seem in retrospect to be rather pretentious.

Some indication of the extent to which the U.O.P.A.'s dual function as protector of its members' working standards and friendly society had been successfully reconciled may be inferred from the Auditors' Report for 1885. Not only had the Association disbursed during the year a total of £2,750 in benefits, including more than £1,100 in sickness benefit, but it had at the same time increased the level of the Reserve Fund—inaugurated only four years earlier—to the figure of £1,384. A firm basis for future expansion was slowly being laid. The Birmingham E.C., as they handed over to Sheffield in 1885, pointed proudly to the increase of 20 Lodges and 584 members, and the addition of £350 to the Reserve Fund, during their three years in office.

CHAPTER IV

THE LATE VICTORIAN YEARS

D URING the early months of 1886 there was a bustle of activity in the Court of the Worshipful Company. After a public meeting in January, when the broad outlines of the registration scheme were described, the Court established its Registration Council with the expressed aim of ensuring that all plumbers in the Metropolitan area should be admitted on production of certificates of competency and evidence of experience at the trade. Although the pilot scheme was confined to London, agreement was also reached to admit plumbers in the provinces. The movement towards registration received the wholehearted approbation of the technical Press and there was a good deal of support for proposals that registration should eventually be made compulsory by statutory legislation. " We fully approve the recommendation of the Plumbers' Company . . ." said *The Health Journal* (March 1886). " We cannot, however, believe that the reform can be completely effected without adequate Parliamentary powers. . . . To advance the three main objects of the move ment, (a) the registration of plumbers, (b) the extension of sound, technical instruction to plumbers, (c) the supervision by the authorities of plumbing work in new buildings, the co-operation of all sanitarians should be heartily offered, for the realisation of these several things would undoubtedly tend largely to promote the public health."

Notwithstanding the flattering tributes paid by the Master of the Worshipful Company to operative plumbers, whom he described as " standing among the crafts in very much the same position that doctors do among the professions," the E.C. were still reluctant to commit themselves in favour of the movement for registration. They did, however, publish fully the reports of various meetings of the Worshipful Company and subsequent reports in the technical Press, " being of the opinion that the matter is of the utmost importance, and demands the consideration of each member." They also repeated at length their grievances against uniformed critics of the plumber and against the deteriorating relationship between employers and apprentices. "There are so many unpractical employers, such as builders, ironmongers, tinsmiths, coppersmiths, slaters, painters, paperhangers, etc., who have commenced to employ plumbers, that we might as well expect a barber to train a boy to pass as a surgeon, or a bricklayer to train a boy to pass as a solicitor, as some of these turn out practical and thorough craftsmen."

Six months later it was a different story. The E.C. were "pleased to note that numerous applications are being made to the Plumbers' Company," and they published further articles from the Press concerning registration, in the hope that "by bringing them direct to the notice of each member, general interest may be aroused in the matter of Registration, because it is better, in our opinion, to prepare for and accept cheerfully, and assist forward to the full extent of our power, a movement that is for the welfare of the trade and the public. Many employers now in their advertisements state that none but R.P.s need apply, also have posted in their shops notice that after such a date workmen who have failed to gain the R.P. will be discharged." This was conversion with a vengeance!

The *Standard* (20th August, 1886) reported that "nearly three hundred plumbers, masters and workmen, have been granted the 'certificate of registration, bearing the company's seal and arms, A.D. 1588,' which is a guarantee of efficiency. No one is called upon to register who was established in business before 1st March, 1886, but he may apply, and on 'satisfactory statement or proof of experience' he will receive the certificate. We may hope . . . that in no long time the uncertified craftsman will find himself out of work."

By the end of the year the number registered had reached the thousand mark, with arrangements being made for registration in several large provincial towns. The E.C. now were completely "sold" on the idea and were urging members "to put forth every effort to improve and perfect themselves. Twenty-five have attended for practical examination—13 failed; and out of 116 who have applied this week, 22 have to attend for practical examination. This will remove the idea that any one that applies can have a certificate. . . ."

The E.C. President, T. Cartwright, was among the guests

E

at the Albion Hotel, Aldersgate, in November when the
Worshipful Company arranged a function attended by the
Lord Mayor and Sheriffs of London and Middlesex.
Responding to a toast, Cartwright said: " The plumbing trade
during the past several years has got into sad disgrace, and
every effort should be made to improve its status. . . ." Never
before in his history had the plumber received so much of
the limelight.

While plumbers were bemused by visions of professional
status and were " casting their thoughts a little higher," more
sombre events underlined the plight of Britain's unemployed.
Monday, 8th February, 1886, became known as " Black
Monday " after rioters from the ranks of a crowd of 20,000 in
Trafalgar Square, attending demonstrations organised by the
Social Democratic Federation, forerunner of the I.L.P., were
prompted by jeering club members in St. James's Street to
express their feelings by smashing the windows of the fashion-
able clubs and shops as they marched to Hyde Park. The
incidents, magnified disproportionately in the Press, caused
something near to panic among the ruling classes. Even
Queen Victoria was moved to protest. " The Queen cannot
sufficiently express her indignation at the monstrous riot,"
she wrote, " which risked people's lives and was a momentary
triumph for Socialism and a disgrace to the capital. If steps,
and very strong ones, are not speedily taken to put these proceedings down with a high hand, to punish severely the *real*
ringleaders . . . the Government will suffer severely."

The Prime Minister, Mr. Gladstone, agreed that the riots
had " stained the reputation of this country in the eyes of the
civilised world." There were two immediate results. A
Mansion House fund for the relief of poverty was boosted
from £3,000 to £70,000 in a few days, and the Metropolitan
Commissioner of Police resigned. More important, however,
was the fact that the attention of the British public had been
drawn sharply to the appalling conditions of the unemployed
in their midst.

Little indication is found in the U.O.P.A. reports of the
dark undercurrents of misery and despair affecting the " sub-
merged tenth " of British citizens. Sympathy was expressed,
however, for American workers who had been on strike for

18 weeks in New York " against the wholesale introduction of labourers into our trade, also to compel the binding of boys for a term of years. We know," said Cherry " that the deterioration of our trade and others dates from the abolishment of guilds and the apprenticeship system." An exchange of correspondence began between Cherry and his American counterpart, Edward Farrell.

The Union's influence continued to increase in the London area with the entry into the U.O.P.A. of three local plumbers' societies: Battersea and South London, the West End Plumbers (taken into London No. 1 Lodge) and Kensington, Chelsea and Notting Hill. Soon afterwards the West Central Plumbers (known as the " White Horse Lodge ") also followed suit, but the East End Lodge maintained their independence.

In spite of continuing pressure from employers for the reduction of working hours and the consequent cutting of weekly wages, the U.O.P.A. managed to avoid any major disasters or conflicts during 1887 and moved slowly but steadily forward in strength of numbers and finance. The year 1888 brought another Delegate Meeting—this time at Montgomery Hall, New Surrey Street, Sheffield. In the interval of five years since the previous D.M. the Association had gained 35 more Lodges and over 1,200 members: this was a remarkable record in the light of economic and trade circumstances of the intervening period. The comparatively low incidence of disputes is shown by the figure of total dispute benefit paid over the five years, only £1,013 as against £5,602 in sickness benefit and £1,535 in funeral benefit.

In his address to the D.M., George Cherry emphasised once again the need for central control and supervision of all Association finance in order that wastage could be reduced to the minimum and reserves strengthened to the maximum. Cherry's foresight was apparent in his appeal to delegates to widen the basis of the U.O.P.A.'s membership by organising " all tradesmen who work in the same shops that we do, and who could, in the event of disputes, do us considerable harm by prolonging the dispute. I do not mean to mix gasfitters, hot water fitters and zinc workers with plumbers, but to keep them separate and distinct. The advantages of such would be most evident in cases of dispute, where employers take advantage of their disorganisation to compel the carrying on of the plumbing work as far as they can."

Unfortunately for the future progress of the Union, Cherry's advice went unheeded. He also submitted a very comprehensive account of the way in which his burden of work had increased; this was to support a proposal before the D.M. that his salary should be raised to £150 a year. Parts of the statement underline his forthright, unequivocal style. On the subject of organising, he said: " The labour of organising a lodge cannot be thoroughly described. It is only by persistent, constant and undaunted effort that they can be organised today, because everything seems against us—bad trade being the principal, and the general quiescent attitude of the employers. When employers are trying to reduce wages, increase hours, and generally encroach upon the freedom and privileges of tradesmen, then they look round for protection. In the absence of these elements, we must get them in with us by all the means at our disposal. We are only as yet, notwithstanding our vast increases, an apology of a society to what we ought to be. I estimate that there are over 20,000 tradesmen in the United Kingdom. Let any one take up a map, and see the vast ranges where we had not lodges or members in the 1882 audit. . . . I know that many think that to go and address a meeting and travel to a place is only a pleasure trip. Any who think so cannot have realised the anxiety of anyone who is going on such an expedition. When I go, whether for one day or one week, I am compelled to stick to my work when I get home so as to make up the arrears."

The Association's initial doubts about the value of the registration movement were nowhere in evidence at the 1888 D.M., when it was unanimously resolved that " this Delegate Meeting, having fully considered the system of registration of qualified plumbers, established by the Worshipful Company of Plumbers, London, deem it worthy of adoption by the Association as a measure necessary in the interest of the trade and the public, and desire that the E.C. do take steps to promote the extension of the system throughout Great

Britain and Ireland, appointing representatives of the Association to act in the matter."

During the year, attempts were being made to recover some of the ground lost in the years of depression. The Leicester E.C. reported that permission had been given to Dundee to apply for an advance of ½d. an hour. " It will be remembered that Dundee submitted to reductions amounting to 1½d. per hour, through bad trade, about eleven years ago; so that if their present application is successful, their wages will be 1d. per hour less than eleven years ago." Disputes were reported from Sheffield and from London—despite the agreement reached in 1887 with the Master Builders' Association.

Most reports of this period, however, were still occupied with accounts of progress in registration: so much so that it may justifiably be said that the Association was obsessed with the notion that registration was the panacea for all its troubles. Trade was slowly picking up and membership was again rising. The Association's first prosecution of a defaulting Lodge Secretary was made under the Trade Union Act of 1871, when the defendant was ordered to repay the sum of about £25 which had been " unlawfully withheld." At long last, the law relating to trade unions appeared to be turning to their advantage.

Early in 1889, Dublin members sought the aid of the Worshipful Company in London to establish a system of technical education and registration for Irish plumbers. Certain elements in the Irish Home Rule Party immediately seized the opportunity to denounce the U.O.P.A. and urge the secession of plumbers in Ireland from the Association. After letters in the Irish press from the secretary of the Worshipful Company's Registration Committee and from George Cherry, declining to " mix plumbing with politics," the issue seems to have died a natural death. Certainly it made little or no impression on the loyalty of the Dublin members.

Incredible as it may now seem, the Association had power in 1889 to open Lodges overseas. In June the E.C. declared that this decision " gives to our brothers who have gone to Buenos Aires the privilege of opening a Lodge there. We hope that the experience gained will be of service to the next Delegate Meeting." The decision had been taken by a Lodge vote and by a remarkably large majority. Exactly how such Lodges were expected to conduct their financial affairs, *vis-à-vis* the parent Association, is not clear. From this point in time one can only express amazement at the inauguration of such far-flung outposts of the U.O.P.A.

Just how far trade unions had come from the black days of the 1820s, when the law was almost entirely punitive to society members, can be appreciated from the report of a court case in Kendal in 1889, when two plumbers " on tramp " from Lancashire were given work by a Kendal master at 6½d. an hour. Soon after commencing work they asked for " country money " (now known as lodging allowance) of 6d. a day as provided for in the U.O.P.A. rules. The employer refused. The two members took the master to court in an attempt to recover the 5s. they claimed. After a fortnight's consideration the Judge issued a postponed judgment. It was in favour of the defendant on the grounds that the sum of 6d. a night was payable only to operatives who were lodging away from home—home meaning in the vicinity of the town where the employer had his business. " They had no home, and were therefore not entitled to it." Dubious logic, perhaps, but at least the results of collective bargaining by organised labour were now being recognised in law, and legal arbitration of this kind was an accomplished fact.

With nearly £1,500 in the Reserve Fund and a membership of over 4,500, the U.O.P.A. entered another decade with a sense of increasing security. Nevertheless, the outlook had its dark corners. In Liverpool, members struck for an increase of a penny an hour in order to maintain parity with members in other parts of the country. " The employers are now complaining of the extravagant and absurd demand for one penny per hour advance," the E.C. commented bitterly, " but when one penny per hour was conceded ten years ago by our members, through arbitration, the amount was then termed reasonable and just." This dispute dragged on for six months in 1890 until at last the Union was obliged to accept the solution of arbitration, which awarded an increase of ½d. an hour but found no justification for reducing working hours from 55 per week.

The dispute on Merseyside was a serious set-back to the

slow but encouraging financial progress of the Association. The E.C. announced the imposition of a weekly levy of 4d. per member but this was withdrawn under pressure from Lodges. The E.C. also issued an appeal for a drastic overhaul of conditions governing payment of incapacitation benefit in order to reduce the drain on funds. At that time the sum of £100 was conditionally available to any member with more than a year's membership who was totally incapacitated from following the trade as the result of industrial accident or disease. Clearly this was an expensive anachronism that could not continue without modification.

Notwithstanding financial pressure, the U.O.P.A. were still ready to give aid to fellow trade unionists in distress. Individual interpretations of the law could still result in swingeing penalties, as was the case of trade unionists at Plymouth who were convicted of intimidation against an employer and fined £20 each or six weeks in gaol. The magistrates' harsh decision found scant support in the Press. Very pointedly, the *Daily Chronicle* declared : " No man has a right to prevent, by personal violence, or the threats of personal violence, any other man from employing whom he will or working for whom he will. But every man has a right to refuse to work for any other man if he chooses; and since each man has this right separately, he does not lose it by joining himself with others in a trade union. . . . It is a serious hardship if the law allows trade union officials to be fined twenty pounds or sent to prison for six weeks for announcing the decision of the union to withdraw the members under certain circumstances. If such an announcement be intimidation, is it not likewise intimidation on the part of an employer to announce that he will discharge the girls working for him if they become members of a trade union? Yet there is not a bench of magistrates in the kingdom which would impose a fine upon any three employers who combined to do this, far less would commit them to prison for six weeks."

In the closing days of 1890 the first important conference between representatives of the U.O.P.A. and the Amalgamated Society of Engineers took place on the question of the allocation of work in the shipbuilding industry. As a result of discussions in Glasgow and Newcastle lasting more than a week, codes of by-laws were drawn up for the apportionment of work between plumbers and engineers at shipbuilding yards in Barrow, Clydeside and Tyneside, which were to endure for many years.

At this time a Lodge vote was taken to determine whether the U.O.P.A. should join the Federation of Engineering and Shipbuilding Trades (forerunner of the Confederation of Shipbuilding and Engineering Unions). By a large majority it was decided to affiliate.

Membership of the Association had risen to over 5,000 by 1890. The Auditors' Report for the year ended March 1891, recorded an increase of 760 new members during the twelve months and the addition of eight Lodges. On the financial side, however, there had been an alarming increase in dispute benefit, which reached a total of nearly £3,000 for the year and outstripped the amount paid in sickness benefit by over £900. The Reserve Fund suffered accordingly and had fallen to a paltry £381 at the end of the financial year. This was trouble with a capital letter.

Understandably, the Delegate Meeting held in May 1891 at the Waterloo Hall in Leicester was largely preoccupied with financial problems. In his report, Cherry said: " The first and most important element of success in procuring and providing for benefits is cash. Our organisation requires thorough overhauling, and placing upon a thoroughly sound footing. It is time the idea was removed that a lodge having met the demands of headquarters, the funds remaining are the lodge's to deal with as they please. Every portion of our expenditure must be governed by rules."

Cherry's arguments were seldom unsupported by facts and figures. He produced a table to show that the Association's finances were far from secure. The average funds per member of ten other trade unions were compared with those of the U.O.P.A., which came bottom of the list with a figure of 18s. 6d. per member, as against £4 4s. 8d. for the Steam Engine Makers, £3 19s. 10d. for the Patternmakers, £3 9s. 1d. for the Engineers and £2 4s. 6d. for the Carpenters and Joiners, the lowest of the ten comparable figures. He also urged the complete revision of the Incapacitation Benefit rule and was critical of the steep increase in strikes with the resultant drain

on funds. More statistical tables revealed that the cost of
disputes in 1890/91 had been no less than 11s. per member—
more than twice the previous peak figure of 5s. 6d. per member for 1881.

Cherry reiterated his pleas for the admission of hot water
fitters, gasfitters, zinc workers and other trades into the Association. " By organising them we should be able to indicate
the line of demarcation between the trades and prevent some
of the condemnation that is so freely bestowed upon us
through the interference with our work by the trades referred
to." In short, if you can't beat 'em, join 'em!

Faced with a massive agenda containing nearly 500 propositions for amendments to rule, it is scarcely surprising that
the 1891 D.M. failed to complete its business. Cherry's
appeals had once again fallen largely on deaf ears. Although
contributions were standardised at 9d. a week and local
variations abolished, the delegates seemed unable to appreciate the Association's precarious financial situation. Incapacitation benefit remained unchanged, strike pay was raised
to 15s. a week, and superannuation benefit was introduced
for members aged 45 and over with a scale of benefit ranging
from 7s. a week for 20 years' membership to 12s. a week for
more than 40 years'. Provision was made, however, for the
Reserve Fund to be maintained at a figure of not less than £1
per member, and entrance fees were increased.

So, too, was George Cherry's salary—at long last: it rose
from £120 to £150 a year. By another decision of the
Leicester D.M., the Association's headquarters returned to its
birthplace—Liverpool, this time on a permanent basis subject
to any further alternative decision by a future D.M.

The first fruits of the Association's decision to join the
Federation of Engineering and Shipbuilding Trades were
harvested during a bitter demarcation dispute at Jarrow. The
dissatisfaction of the Engineers in one particular shipyard
with the recently concluded agreement on apportionment of
work came to a head with their demand for a separate
" plant " agreement. as a result, U.O.P.A. members were
locked out. " We have, thanks to the influence of the Federation," the E.C. reported, " been able to resist the power of
one of the largest trade societies and employers combined."

Shortly after the conclusion of the 1891 D.M. the Federation of E. and S. Trades held its first annual meeting in Manchester. The U.O.P.A. was represented by George Cherry and a Barrow member, John Geddes. The dispute between engineers and plumbers at Jarrow was discussed in detail and the A.S.E. was urged by the Federation to accept arbitration to reach a settlement of the dispute. Cherry also asked the delegate from the Ironfounders Society for an assurance that plumbers would not be enrolled into that organisation. It is apparent that the organising activities of various unions (especially in engineering and shipbuilding) were beginning to overlap and to produce the regrettable element of competitiveness between unions that has created so many " poaching " problems in more modern times.

The second half of 1891 was notable for the secession of four more Scottish Lodges—Aberdeen, Coatbridge, Dundee and Edinburgh, with a total strength of about 350 members. Efforts made by George Cherry were partially successful in maintaining the Association's links with Aberdeen and Dundee. The U.O.P.A. of Scotland (established as a result of the first Scottish secession in 1872) absorbed most of the disgruntled members. Raymond Postgate makes the following comment: " More interesting than the detailed history of this small organisation (the Scottish society) are the reasons for this fissiparous tendency of Scottish plumbers. The English society at one time had probably more than half its whole membership in engineering and shipbuilding, and not in building at all, while the Scottish association had no more than sixty ship plumbers all told. It was universally felt in Scotland that the English association neglected the interests of the building section for others, and spent the money and time of the association in conflicts in shipbuilding and engineering, where in the nature of things it counted for very little, and the money was as good as wasted. In the second place, the habits of Scottish plumbers differed. The invasion of the general master-builder had gone much less far than in England. Master-plumbers and master-plumbers' associations counted for much more. Employment was consequently much more regular—many of the members of the Scottish association had worked in the one shop the better part of their lives. On the basis of less unemployment, a Scottish society could pay higher benefits for the same subscription as the English, and the temptation to accept the industrial weakness with the financial profit so secured was too great to be resisted."

Meanwhile, the campaign for the statutory registration of plumbers continued to receive firm support and widespread publicity. In October 1891, the Clerk to the Worshipful Company addressed a public meeting in Belfast Town Hall on the subject. Eight members of the U.O.P.A. now sat on the Company's Registration Committee, and the Association's President (still Thomas Anderton of Liverpool) again spoke at a banquet given by the Worshipful Company in December. He declared: " It is the bounden duty of everyone in sympathy with the movement for registering plumbers to see that none are employed unless they are registered."

The year 1892 opened with " signs of labour wars on every side." The E.C. were urging moderation in trade disputes (" A little conciliatory talk will in some cases prevent serious disputes ") while at the same time they launched a violent attack on the Engineers for their " slanderous, lying and malicious statements " and also announced that " through the prompt action of the officers and members of (East London) Lodge, our members caught a brassfinisher trying to solder a half-inch pipe into a W.C. soil pipe." Conciliation might be they keynote in relations with employers, but for other trade unions it was the " big stick." At Swansea and Sunderland employers were persuaded " not to allow black-smiths to interfere with gasfitting," while a shop at Barrow was blacked because " a painter was permitted to interfere with plumbing."

A protracted strike at Cardiff, involving all building trades but joiners, was in its second month. The report of this dispute is interesting insofar as it reflects on the one hand the confused attitude of the U.O.P.A. leaders towards united action by building workers, and on the other hand their undoubted clarity of vision in forecasting future difficulties if the ranks of the U.O.P.A. were not opened to ancillary workers. Speaking of the Cardiff dispute, the report began: " We could have made arrangements some weeks ago but to have done so we should have broken an agreement arrived at by the Federation of Building Trades that all trades stand together. . . We are of the opinion that our brothers would have obtained the whole of their demands before now, but for the fact that the employers are being considerably relieved by the hot water fitters. This action emphasises the necessity for admitting hot water fitters into our Association. We have often pointed out the danger of this trade remaining disorganised and being used by employers in times of dispute to overcome us. There are in some parts of the country plumbers, glaziers, hot water fitters, and gasfitters, each a separate trade, but all were at one time generally combined in one. The sooner we recognise this growing danger and cope with it, the better. We can do so now, but if it grows much more we shall be unable to deal with it."

The Cardiff strike continued. In September it was reported that " Mr. Graeme Hunter, the self-styled ' Champion Trades Union Smasher,' three months ago undertook to supply all employers with as many men or substitutes as they needed. There must be a leak somewhere, because as fast as men arrive they go again, notwithstanding such attractions as a barracks, where birds of a feather are caged, and an escort of police, beer and Sankey's hymns, *ad lib*." At the end of the year, reporting the separate settlement with the Cardiff Master Plumbers, the E.C. added a bitter comment: " After our members had been out five months we wrote to the E.C.s of the trades in dispute to try and arrange for a Conference . . . at Cardiff. In one case we are yet waiting for a reply, and in two cases the replies were such that will not warrant us to presume to address such august bodies again. In future we will not undertake to stand out till other trades secure such terms as they want. If we can obtain satisfactory terms, we shall accept them."

The figure for dispute benefit for the year 1892 again topped the £3,000 mark and was the largest single item of benefit expenditure.

Nor was 1893 a happy year for the U.O.P.A. A long dispute at Blackburn, where local employers refused to countenance federated action in support of the Plasterers, made further inroads into the Association's reserves. Once more the Plumbers stood firmly with the Federation although with little enthusiasm for a dispute which, so far as the U.O.P.A. was concerned, was simply a repetition of the costly affair at Cardiff. The E.C. also found themselves under attack by Birkenhead Lodge for their refusal to let U.O.P.A. members take employment at the shipyard of Laird Brothers, where gasfitters were being engaged on the plumbing work for H.M.S. *Royal Oak* and other new naval vessels. The E.C. argued that members would have to work in Laird's yard for 3s. 6d. a week less than the standard rate on Merseyside, thus giving local employers a heaven-sent opportunity to seek general wage reductions. Moreover, plumbers entering the yard would lose their status of " plumbers " and would be scheduled as gasfitters, thereby sacrificing the support and protection afforded them by virtue of the U.O.P.A.'s affiliation to the Federation of E. and S. Trades.

Trouble also blew up in Scotland between the two Societies when the Scottish U.O.P.A. insisted on joint action against plumbers employed by the Caledonian Railway Company who were refusing to abide by jointly agreed by-laws. The U.O.P.A. expelled at least one member only to find that the Scottish association refused to take action against its own offenders. Ultimately the dispute was referred to a Disputes Committee of the Glasgow Trades Council, who recommended that an apology be sent by the Scottish society and a joint meeting be held to find ways and means of avoiding future problems of this kind.

By far the largest shadow on the horizon at this time, however, was the increasing fragmentation of the work formerly accepted as that of one man: the plumber. At the end of 1893, acting on a resolution from Newcastle upon Tyne Lodge which requested a vote on the association on the admittance of gasfitters, hot water fitters and zinc workers, the E.C. issued a long circular in an attempt to persuade the members that they must now come to terms with reality. " Within the memory of the majority of members our trade has undergone some radical changes. Generally, a wholesale disintegration is taking place, and each part added to some other, or a special trade created. We now find that gasfitting is a separate trade; the gasfitters are generally employed by master plumbers. In many cases firms have sprung into existence with high-sounding titles such as ' Domestic and Sanitary Engineers.' These have created a new class of workmen, who are now doing a quantity of the hot-water work, such as taking the supplies direct to baths, basins, sinks, etc., and in many cases they fix the W.C.s, soil pipes, etc. The reason why gasfitters and hot-water fitters are employed to do this class of work is obvious—their wages are less, considerably less in some cases, than those of the plumbers."

The E.C. repeated George Cherry's appeal to the 1883 D.M. and concluded by declaring: " We have ample evidence that a society has been formed for the purpose of uniting the gas and hot-water fitters, and a fair number have joined. We can fight the ' devil better chained than loose.' While they are organised—if we permit them to organise apart from us—then we shall have to deal with and probably fight them, at tremendous cost, as we had to fight the engineers. We give way to no one in our pride for the trade, but we cannot allow our pride to lead us to complete disintegration and destruction."

These were strong words: looking back from a distance of 70 years it is hard to imagine that anyone would disagree with the sound commonsense of the E.C.'s arguments. Be that as it may, time has certainly confirmed their premonitions. But the members remained adamant, and rejected the proposed dilution of the Association by an overwhelming majority. The voting was about 1,250 to 350.

According to rule, another Lodge vote was taken in 1894 to decide whether a Delegate Meeting should be held. The result of this one, too, could hardly have been received with approbation by the E.C. Fifty-four Lodges recorded 109 votes in favour, while 67 Lodges against a D.M. could muster only 96 votes. Preston Lodge had already suggested that propositions and amendments to rule should be dealt with in the Lodges at specially summoned meetings; while the

E.C., accepting the inevitability of a D.M. in 1895, warned that a levy of 2s. a member should be made to keep costs to the minimum. They also put forward a compromise suggestion made by George Cherry: let the D.M. take place, but limit the full meeting to three or four days and appoint a 14-man committee from the D.M. delegates to deal with unfinished business.

This last suggestion was adopted and the Delegate Meeting was held at the Daulby Hall, Liverpool. In his report, Cherry revealed that during the term of the Liverpool E.C. an average of £504 had been paid in strike benefit each quarter. Emphasising the need for conciliation and a policy of give-and-take, he again referred to the incursions of other tradesmen into the work of the plumber and repeated his plea for the admission of ancillary workers into the U.O.P.A. " The time of this meeting would be well spent in agreeing upon a general policy for the protection of our trade interests; if not, there will be very little trade left for us. Each quarterly report contains records of attempts to encroach upon our trade by Carpenters, Smiths, Brass-finishers, Plasterers, Slaters, Gas and Hot-Water Fitters." Cherry's concluding appeal was concerned with the Asso-ciation's finances. " The living from hand to mouth is exceedingly dangerous. The danger of some places being in dispute, especially London, has cost me many sleepless nights and anxious days. I do hope this meeting will lay the foundation of a financial system that will place this Associa-tion in a position second to none."

In the event, the 1895 D.M. which, after a fully-attended session lasting six days, resolved itself into a committee of 15 to complete the agenda, accomplished very little of major consequence. A suggestion for the establishment of District Committees was rejected on grounds of expense. The per-manency of Liverpool as Association headquarters was terminated; the U.O.P.A. moved into Garnet Hill, Glasgow, and was governed during the ensuing years by a Scottish Executive Council. George Cherry was given an Assistant General Secretary for the first time, and his son, Tom H. Cherry, was elected to the new office.

In their report for 1895, the Association's auditors were of the opinion " that the general question of finance is one calling for the serious consideration of the Association, and think it unfortunate that the D.M. did not adopt some of the proposals laid before them with a view to placing this matter on a more equitable basis."

Relations between the U.O.P.A. and the Scottish society were not improved by a Court action early in 1896 when a member of the latter sued a U.O.P.A. member for £10 damages. Members of the U.O.P.A. working for a firm in Port Glasgow had been receiving 8½d. an hour when they discovered that the plaintiff had been engaged at a rate of 7d. an hour. They demanded that the employer should either pay the Scottish member the full rate or dismiss him. Through some misunderstanding the U.O.P.A. members failed to return to work and the employer dismissed the plaintiff. The Scottish member won his action. This, of course, was seventy years or so before the issue of Rookes v. Barnard reverberated through the British trade union movement.

Proposals for the statutory registration of plumbers were finally laid before the House of Commons in the form of the Plumbers' Registration Bill, 1896—ten years after the movement had been launched with such vociferous gusto. The matter had, in fact, already been under discussion in a Select Committee of the Commons and a Bill had been ordered to be printed as far back as 1892. Even in those distant days it must have been apparent that statutory registration was not likely to be achieved overnight.

During 1896 the E.C. were in conference with two important organisations. They met the London Master Builders' Association in May and were successful in laying the basis for a new Working Rule Agreement providing, among other things, for disputes to be referred to a Conciliation Board. The E.C. also announced that the Master Plumbers had formed a national association. " At their meetings their intentions, and ability to carry out their intentions, of boycotting members of this Association have been freely expressed. It is possible that they intend to carry on a guerilla warfare, attacking us in several directions at once, thereby crippling our funds and rendering us helpless to resist them."

Notwithstanding this unpromising welcome to the new employers' association, three months later the E.C. reported an approach from the Master Plumbers offering suggestions for the formation of a Board of Reference " to consider any question affecting the plumbing trade and to procure the improvement of any existing laws, usages and customs which the Board may consider to be prejudicial to the trade . . . and to promote and secure an honourable and equitable adjustment of any matter or question pending between employer and employed, with a view of avoiding or preventing strikes, lock-outs or other measures which prove disastrous to our mutual interests."

The E.C. ignored the harsh things they had said in their previous report and referred the Master Plumbers' proposals to the members, even going so far as to include amendments they had already put forward to the original overtures. As in the case of registration ten years earlier, the E.C. demonstrated that they were still agile enough to perform a back somersault in the interval between two quarterly reports. Perhaps the reason for their change of heart can be perceived in the comments made on the result of the Lodge vote which approved the setting up of a Board of Reference: " You have decided to agree to such. This we regard as a step in the right direction. We hope and expect the meetings with the employers will result in avoiding serious disputes, hence avoid loss to members, the Association, and the employers." The operatives' side of the Board was to comprise two E.C. and three lay members.

The Plumbers were clearly convinced that conciliation would be a far more profitable proposition than militancy— especially under the old-fashioned system of the U.O.P.A. Their judgment must also have been coloured by the none-too-healthy state of the Association's finances. In 1896, dispute benefit was again a major item of expenditure, accounting for more than twice the amount paid to E.C. Officers, including miscellaneous expenses. In the returns for March 1897, the E.C. warned Lodges that they would not consent " to them coming out on strike till the conditions specified in General Rule 39 are complied with, viz., if the employers will not meet a deputation collectively in conference, then deputa-

F

tions must wait upon each employer and ascertain what objections, if any, they have to the proposed changes. Some lodges seem to be under the impression that when a notice is sent to the employers, it is their duty to wait till the notice expires, then come out on strike. Members should not delude themselves with the idea that if they come out they will not be out one week. Once a strike has commenced, the most experienced cannot foretell when it will end."

All unions affiliated to the Federation of E. and S. Trades were asked in May 1897, to take a vote of their members on the question of a reduced working week. With the main question, three alternative figures for working hours were put forward: 51 hours, 48, and 45. It may seem strange to the twentieth-century trade unionist that there should be any need for such a referendum at all: but it is even stranger to note that members of the U.O.P.A. voted in favour of a 48-hour week—rather to the annoyance of the Executive Council, who argued very strongly in favour of a 51-hour week (*after* the result of the vote was known), mainly on the grounds that this would allow two daily meal breaks and would reduce the time lost by members who missed the 6 a.m. start. Such glimpses of labour questions occupying the minds of trade union leaders at the turn of the century must surely confound the modern worker who imagines that demands for the 40-hour week originate in the pre-history of organised labour.

Throughout 1897 a serious dispute in the engineering industry threatened the livelihood of many U.O.P.A. members. The craft unions, including the Plumbers, showed some irritation when they were accused of giving only half-hearted support to the " allied trades " involved in the dispute. Undoubtedly the older unions were still rather unsympathetic towards the larger, " amalgamated " societies that had sprung up in the 1860s. The spirit of working-class unity generated in the black years of the " document " had largely evaporated: trade unionism was now respectable, and out of familiarity grew contempt—the contempt of an artisan class for the unskilled labourers, the " navvies " and all those unfortunates who had not been privileged to rise to the dignified ranks of craftsmen. In fairness it must be admitted that this attitude prevailed no less among members of the U.O.P.A. than those of other craft organisations; it was reflected in the increasing intolerance of any encroachments on traditional work of the plumber, and it certainly had a retarding effect on the growth and development of the union.

On the advice of the Executive that the Association was not " at present able to bear the expenditure," members voted by a slender margin not to hold the Delegate Meeting due in 1899 under the rules. They also decided that the U.O.P.A. should not affiliate to the General Federation of Trade Unions, an organisation sponsored by the T.U.C. for the purpose of securing united industrial action by existing trade associations. The objects of the G.F.T.U. were " to uphold the rights of combination of labour; to improve in every direction the general position and status of the workers; the consolidation of labour as a whole, and to secure unity of action amongst all Societies forming the Federation." The organisation, according to the Webbs, arose " out of the losses caused by the costly engineering dispute of 1897-98 " and was " designed exclusively as a mutual reinsurance agency against the heavy financial burden to which, in the form of strike pay . . . labour disputes subject every active trade society."

The circular issued by the E.C. inviting U.O.P.A. members to vote on the scheme was hardly impartial : " We note that many unpleasant names are conferred gratis upon the E.C.s of various Societies because they do not, at the bidding of each adventurer who presents an apparently laudable and gullible paper scheme, hand over their funds. We at any rate claim to be of the rank and file, and better Trade Unionists, and have a longer record than many who are so free with their abuse. We acknowledge no leaders. We think for ourselves, and work daily at our trade, and have with you paid our mites to build up a Reserve Fund which will not at any time with our consent go out of this Association's control. To help build up a Political machine—this is the aim of most of the schemes."

Following a lock-out of plasterers by members of the

National Association of Master Builders for alleged "restrictive practices," the Masters sent an "impertinent" letter to the other building unions asking for an assurance that they would not support the plasterers in any way, on the threat of a general lock-out. A meeting was held in Derby in June 1899, when George Cherry as secretary of the building trade representatives joined with three other union leaders in a meeting with the Master Builders to try to arrange a general conference. The Masters' terms were totally unacceptable and the unions were left to put forward proposals for discussion. At a further meeting in Manchester, where the U.O.P.A. was represented by John H. Edmiston, later to become the Union's General Secretary, proposed rules were drafted for a Board of Conciliation. Mr. W. S. Hilton of the N.F.B.T.O., in *Foes to Tyranny,* remarks: "The constitution suggested was, on a great number of points, similar to that of the present National Joint Council for the Building Industry. At a meeting between national representatives of the major unions and employers on 27th July, 1899 . . . agreement was reached to proceed with the formation of a conciliation board almost entirely along the lines of the draft put forward by the unions. It looked, for a short time, as if both men and masters were poised for a really progressive and major advance in industrial relationships."

Optimism was short-lived. At the eleventh hour the employers insisted on a "monetary guarantee" that the Conciliation Board's decisions would be carried out—in short, a system of fines for non-observance. When this spanner was thrown in by the Master Builders (as a face-saving device to allow the scheme to collapse, some unions alleged) the U.O.P.A. and several other organisations had already voted for acceptance of the Conciliation Board. In the light of the employers' unreasonable demands, however, the scheme was still-born.

On the domestic front, the closing months of the nineteenth century found General Office on the move once more, after a vote taken in lieu of a decision by a Delegate Meeting. Manchester was chosen this time; the U.O.P.A. headquarters were duly established in Upper Brook Street. To deal with the propositions and amendments to rules which normally would have been handled by the D.M., a committee was elected of representatives from 21 districts into which the Union had been arbitrarily divided to break down the membership into groups each of approximately 500 members. After it had considered all the proposed amendments, this " Rules Revision Committee," as it became known, would make recommendations to be accepted or rejected by a ballot vote of the members of the Association. Rather a complicated process, no doubt—but cheaper than a Delegate Meeting.

For the United Operative Plumbers' Association, the century ended amid a bustle of activity. They could look back on their thirty-five years' existence as a national society with no small degree of satisfaction. Severe storms had been weathered successfully and in spite of many petty irritations, mostly attributable, they considered, to the activities of other trade unions, the Association was still making numerical and financial progress. Membership topped the 10,000 mark early in 1899 and during the year there was a net gain of 718 members. There were 184 Lodges. It was indeed a far cry from the handful of Lodges with less than 900 members who appeared on the Union's first report in 1866.

CHAPTER V

INTO THE TWENTIETH CENTURY

AMONG the twenty-one members elected as a Rules Revision Committee in 1900 were two Scotsmen who were later to achieve high office in the U.O.P.A.— Edward Ellis Burns of Glasgow No. 1 Lodge and Lachlan MacDonald of Glasgow No. 2. The Committee was in session from 4th to 12th June. Its recommendations arising from the proposals it had to consider from Lodges were many and varied, but among the most important was a new rule providing for the election of a General Council of fourteen members, elected from an equal number of divisions of the union each with approximately the same membership. This General Council of lay members would meet once a year, or when summoned by the E.C., and would have power to abrogate E.C. decisions. The Council was to function quite separately from the E.C., established in 1876 and increased in number to eleven at the 1888 Delegate Meeting. The practice of employing full-time officers to manage the day-to-day affairs of the society, while providing at the same time a body of lay members to act as arbiters, had already been adopted by other trade unions, including the Carpenters and Joiners. The arrangement may appear to have been somewhat cumbersome, but it was clearly the origin of two particular sections of the machinery of our present union: District Committees and the Final Appeal Court. It was also the intention, however, that the General Council would supplement the Delegate Meeting, to be held in future only once in every six years, subject to endorsement by Lodge vote. The Council was therefore to serve a three-fold purpose: to act as a kind of permanent Rules Revision Committee, as the final arbiter in disputes over E.C. decisions, and to ensure that the U.O.P.A. had an authoritative body that was truly "national" in its composition. The E.C., it will be recalled, were at that time chosen from among the members of the Lodge or Lodges in whatever town the Union currently had its headquarters. The new rule also proposed that each division represented on the General Council should elect its own District Auditor.

The R.R.C. recommended that contributions be increased from 9d. to 1s. a week and that the Reserve Fund minimum be raised to £3 per member. Benefits were extended by the re-introduction of out-of-work benefit at the rate of 1s. 6d. a day for full members. Originally provided for in the 1865 rules, this benefit was abolished as a national liability at the 1873 D.M.

The Union's legal aid scheme for members injured at work also has its origins in the 1900 R.R.C.'s recommendations. It was proposed that a grant of up to £20 should be made, at the discretion of the E.C., to defray legal expenses incurred by any member who contested an action under the comparatively new Workmen's Compensation Act.

After some delay caused by confusion over methods of voting, the R.R.C.'s recommendations were finally approved by the members and became effective in April 1901.

The Workmen's Compensation Act, 1897, was the first step in a long series of Parliamentary statutes, culminating in the Industrial Injuries Act, 1946 and subsequent amending legislation, designed to protect workers against financial loss and to compensate for " pain and suffering " resulting from accidents at work. The U.O.P.A. reports of 1900 show that the Act was by no means regarded as perfect; efforts were soon being made to remove some of its obvious anomalies. Nevertheless, not only was it an important landmark in the process of labour legislation, but it also had a marked effect on the attitude of employers towards the safety of their workpeople, since there was no provision under the Act for an employer to " contract out," as there had been under the old Employers' Liability Act. Three compensation settlements for U.O.P.A. members were reported in December: the sums ranged from five guineas to £30 and the cases had all been settled out of court *after* E.C. authority had been given to commence proceedings against the employers.

The year 1901 was very significant in the history of British labour. The previous year had seen the creation of the Labour Representation Committee, stemming from a resolution passed at the 1899 T.U.C. in the following terms: " That this Congress having regard to its decisions in former years and with a view to securing a better representation of the interests of Labour in the House of Commons hereby instructs the Parliamentary Committee to invite the co-operation of all the co-operative, socialistic, trade union and other working-class organisations to jointly co-operate on lines mutually agreed upon, in convening a special congress of representatives from such of the above-named organisations as may be willing to take part to devise ways and means for securing the return of an increased number of Labour members to the next Parliament."

At the subsequent congress at the Memorial Hall, Farringdon Street, London, the L.R.C. was launched—but without the support of the Co-operative Movement, the influential Miners' Federation, and many other large trade unions, who regarded the new venture into politics with undisguised scepticism.

The birth of the British Labour Party went unheralded in the annals of the U.O.P.A. Domestic affairs were probably too pressing to permit much attention being paid to the historic events then taking place. Unemployment was higher than usual, the rule book was being laboriously revised, and, as we have already noted, the U.O.P.A. were not exactly in the vanguard of politically active societies. The need for more Labour representation in Parliament, however, was suddenly and dramatically underlined in 1901 by the famous " Taff Vale Judgment " of the House of Lords.

The trouble began with a small dispute in South Wales involving members of the Amalgamated Society of Railway Servants on the one hand and the Taff Vale Railway Company on the other. The introduction of " blacklegs " by the Company's impetuous General Manager led to lively clashes between the strikers and their non-union opponents. The Manager lost his temper and sued the Amalgamated Society for damages for losses incurred as a result of the strike.

No one, least of all the Company's legal advisers, thought he would succeed in anything except making a fool of himself. The trade union legislation of 1871 and 1875 had deliberately refrained from giving unions the legal status of corporate bodies, with the obvious but unwritten intention of making it impossible to sue them for damages. In such circumstances, the decision of the Law Lords (to whom the case was eventually pressed by the Taff Vale Company's Manager) dumbfounded everyone, including the legal profession. Damages of £23,000 were awarded against the A.S.R.S., plus costs of £19,000.

Francis Williams, in his fine book *Magnificent Journey,* makes the following comments: " For more than a quarter of a century, ever since the Trade Union Act of 1871 and the successful outcome of the campaign against the Criminal Law Amendment Act in 1875, the trade unions had rested secure in the belief that the days of their outlawry were over and that whatever the economic hazards that faced them this at least was certain: their business of collective bargaining had behind it the full protection of the law even if it should be necessary to force an industrial issue to a strike. Now this assurance was suddenly destroyed . . . by the Taff Vale decision. The whole legal foundation on which trade union activities in industrial disputes had been conducted since the trade unions had won their struggle for legal recognition was thus swept away overnight by a decision that ran completely contrary to the long-settled interpretation of the laws affecting trade unions. At one stroke the whole system of collective bargaining upon which trade unionism depended was undermined and the threat to take combined action in defence of wages robbed of its power."

The trade unions looked aghast on the reflection of their own legal nakedness and woke up to the harsh reality of the fact that only by creating strong Parliamentary representation could they hope to recover their statutory decency. As a result, the L.R.C.'s effective affiliated trade union membership rose meteorically from 353,000 spread over 41 unions (1900) to nearly a million in 165 unions (1903). After a comparatively quiet delivery the infant Labour Party heard its first banshee and began to scream its head off.

The Executive Council of the U.O.P.A. greeted 1902 with a declaration in bold type to the effect that owing to the " uncertain state of the law," unless they were previously consulted and had given their consent they would not be responsible for any action of their officers and members.

At the same time they expressed deep concern at the run on Association funds by payment of out-of-work benefit and issued stern warnings about the qualifications for benefit and methods of payment.

Perhaps it would be unkind to deprecate the absence of comments from U.O.P.A. headquarters on national events in 1902, in view of the Plumbers' preoccupation with a domestic tragedy which must have made them temporarily insensible to all else. On 7th August, George Cherry died at the age of 51. After attending a routine Executive meeting on Tuesday, he became unconscious in the early hours of Wednesday and died on Thursday morning. For his colleagues it must have been almost an impossibility to visualise the United Operative Plumbers' Association minus George Baker Cherry: in the words of the E.C.: " His long experience with the Association (having nursed it from childhood to manhood) gave him a perfect mastery of every detail and enabled him to readily solve complications to which many of us would need to give long and deep thought. Above suspicion, he was always kind and ready to assist the needy, even to the extent of injuring himself financially. His whole thought was the welfare of the Association, and his sterling qualities made for him a large circle of friends. . . . He has left an example worthy of imitation both of character and all that which is noble."

George Cherry had led the U.O.P.A. for 23 years—longer than any other General Secretary before or after him. He had been fearless in attack and implacable in defence. Repeatedly he had voiced his opinions in a forthright and unequivocal manner and although many of his warnings and exhortations had gone unheeded he had created deep respect by his utterance of them. Under Cherry's leadership the number of Lodges had risen from 61 to 195 and membership from 2,384 to 11,270. In 1879, when he took office, the Association's quarterly expenditure had been £545 and its cash balance was £340; at the time of his death these figures were £5,029 and £21,749 respectively.

Until elections could be held for a new G.S., Cherry's duties were taken over by John H. Edmiston, secretary of

Manchester No. 2 Lodge and member of the Manchester Executive Council.

On the first ballot paper there were 23 candidates, including Edmiston himself and Lachlan MacDonald. The first count eliminated only three contestants, and faced with the possibility of repeated ballots the E.C. decided that the " clear majority " system should be applied on the second ballot. This meant that only those candidates who together polled a majority of the votes should go to the country again. The outcome was a contest between Edmiston and E. E. Burns of Glasgow No. 1. Burns was the victor by nearly a thousand votes and took up his duties on 16th December, 1902.

The death of Cherry was the beginning of the most disreputable period in the Union's history. Trade was deteriorating rapidly and reductions in wages were being enforced all over the country. The movement for statutory registration, initiated so enthusiastically in 1885, was dying an agonising death in Parliament. The Registration Bill had passed through the House of Lords (where it might have been most expected to falter) with the support of local government representatives, but had been violently opposed at every turn in the Commons " by the Ironmongers," the E.C. announced, " through an agitation got up by their Journal. The agitation seems to have been pretty much a move for advertising the paper, by means of sending over the country petitions for signature against the Bill. About 2,000 signatures were thus obtained, but, as far as we can learn, the bulk of them were those of persons having no interest whatever in the Plumbing trade, many of them not known even by name to any of our members, and having nothing to do with Plumbing beyond selling water taps, or a bath occasionally, and employing a handy man to fix it." The E.C. suggested that a counter petition in support of the Bill should be launched.

Unemployment among U.O.P.A. members in the early part of 1903 was running at the level of 7 per cent with no sign of improvement. Disputes with other unions over encroachments on plumbers' work were increasing, so much so that the E.C. devoted considerable space to the problem in the March returns, suggesting once again that the solution lay (as George Cherry had repeatedly declared) in the admission into the

U.O.P.A. of kindred trades. Though the intent was similar, the E.C.'s approach was noticeably less forceful than Cherry's had been: " We would probably be creating a better safeguard for our trade interests by taking those trades in with us and raising them to our own level, than by wasting our own and their means in fighting against each other."

More organised resistance by employers in the Commons resulted in the rejection of the Trades Dispute Bill, a measure introduced by trade union M.P.s to rectify the deficiencies, so startlingly revealed by the Taff Vale decision, in existing trade union law. As the Master Builders declared in their journal: " Had it not been for the Employers' Parliamentary Council, it is quite possible that the fate of the Bill would have been different." This event again underlined the urgent need for trade unions to strengthen the links with the Labour Representation Committee, which had just announced the establishment of a fund for the maintenance of Labour Members in the House of Commons and to assist in paying election charges. All unions were invited to contribute. On motions submitted to the E.C. by Bournemouth and Southampton Lodges, the question of the U.O.P.A.'s affiliation to the L.R.C. was put before the members, who gave a favourable verdict. The amount of the political levy was set as 1s. per member per annum.

Until the turn of the century, that section of the quarterly report dealing with local disputes had consisted mainly of summaries of the efforts being made up and down the country to improve wages and working conditions or to resist the employers' attempts to debase them. By 1903 the picture was quite different. Each quarter the section on disputes was filled almost entirely with reports of squabbles with slaters, fitters, tinsmiths, plasterers, engineers, hot-water fitters, brassfinishers, whitesmiths, zincworkers, electricians, bricklayers, carpenters, painters—in fact, with nearly every trade associated even remotely with the building process. No wonder Raymond Postgate was moved to comment: " One craft in these sectional quarrels attained a frightful pre-eminence. The plumbers became the Ishmaels of the building world."

Harsh words, maybe: but the records bear witness to their underlying truth. Had George Cherry remained in command the story might have been a different one, but the E.C. appeared to pin their faith on approaches made to the National Association of Master Plumbers, with the object of joint action being taken against " poaching," and to the Royal Institute of British Architects " in an endeavour to secure their approval to the work we claim as plumbers." These meetings did, indeed, prove partially successful in the short-term objectives and brought some alleviation of conflict in isolated cases. But the problem was far too serious to be solved by such " off-beat " measures.

During 1904 the E.C. also found themselves in conflict with the City and Guilds of London Institute over the constitution and functions of the Institute's Advisory Committee in Plumbers' Work. Hand in hand with the Worshipful Company, the U.O.P.A. had submitted proposals for plumbing examinations which the Institute had rejected. So far as technical education was concerned, it appeared to the E.C. that they were better served by continuing their alliance with the Worshipful Company and the Master Plumbers. The Executive also clashed with Central London Lodge, where a member had been allowed " to work contrary to General Rules " and local by-laws. On refusing to obey the E.C.'s instructions to penalise the member concerned, the Lodge was summarily disbanded and its funds, by application to the Registrar of Friendly Societies, transferred to the U.O.P.A.

In the same year the General Secretary, himself a Glaswegian, made an abortive attempt to achieve fusion between the U.O.P.A. and the Scottish Society. Not only did the latter refuse point-blank to entertain what they termed a " preposterous proposal," but this move by Burns touched off such an explosion between the two societies that the noise reverberated throughout the kingdom. A proposed reduction of $\frac{1}{2}$d. an hour by Glasgow employers was resisted by members of the U.O.P.A. but accepted by the Scottish Society: in the resulting confusion some 400 members of the U.O.P.A. were on strike for about six months and the Scottish Society was subsequently expelled from the Glasgow Trades Council. The *Glasgow Weekly Herald* (6th May, 1905) had the following comment: " What a lesson in combination has the lamentable

quarrel between the two Plumbers' Societies in our city fur-
nished us. Here are two bodies—one comparatively insigni-
ficant, with hardly any funds at its disposal, and the other of a
national character, ably managed, with its credit good for
borrowing powers if necessary. . . . Then comes a demand by
the employers for the reduction of a halfpenny an hour and
other alterations in the working by-laws. If there is anything
which distinguishes between the tactics of a body of ' blacklegs ' and a body professing to be Trade Unionists . . . it is
that in the first instance each individual fights for his own
hand regardless of his fellows; and in the second instance, in
face of a common danger, forget petty differences in the desire
to present a united front, with the object of retaining their
present wages and conditions of employment. What a
spectacle for gods and men, then, had we on Labour Day!
On the one hand were some 200 men working away on the
employers' terms; on the other were 400 men on strike, not
only as a protest against a reduction, but also with the greater
object of assisting employers who were willing to continue
the old terms to another 400 men. So you see you have at
least 800 men involved in a dispute which possibly would
have been avoided altogether had the members of the lesser
society acted the manly part that is generally associated with
the principles of Trade Unionism. And the irony of the
position will be further accentuated should those on strike
succeed in defeating the demands of the employers, as, of
course, those presently working at reduced rates will presumably have no objection to reverting to the old rate of
wages which others have fought for. A more miserable story
of selfishness I have not read for many a day. . . ."

The troubles confronting the Executive Council of the
U.O.P.A. in 1905 must have seemed endless. A year earlier,
following the customary procedure, propositions and amendments to rule had been assembled and considered by the
General Council, whose recommendations were published by
the E.C. with the intention that a straightforward Lodge vote
should determine their fate. But the E.C. were soon dis-

illusioned. With the requisite support, Dublin Lodge demanded that a Delegate Meeting be held to deal with the proposed amendments. When the vote on a Delegate Meeting was finally taken it became quite clear that the U.O.P.A. members had had enough of " government by committee "; they endorsed the proposal to hold a D.M. by the massive majority of 3,350 to 664. They also insisted that the meeting would deal with the original propositions and amendments— not with the General Council's recommendations, as suggested by the E.C.

After an interval of ten years, U.O.P.A. delegates assembled once again in February 1905, for the tenth Delegate Meeting, held at the Co-operative Hall, Downing Street, Ardwick, Manchester. The net result of ten days' talking was not very substantial. At the instigation of London Lodges acting in concert, a brake was applied to the accelerating outflow of funds in the form of out-of-work benefit: the qualification of 12 months' contributions before eligibility for benefit was inserted in the rule. Possibly the two most sensible changes made in 1905 were those that brought the Association back on to familiar lines from which it had departed some years earlier: future Delegate Meetings would be held according to rule (without the equivocation of a vote), and the General Council, with its rather ambiguous functions and powers, was abolished. A move by Manchester Lodges for the centralisation of the Association's funds was defeated. London was named as the next headquarters of the U.O.P.A., and members of the Executive Council were to be elected from Lodges within a 12-mile radius of General Office.

There still existed in the Association a good deal of opposition towards the decision to affiliate to the Labour Representation Committee and to impose a levy on all members. The E.C. regretted to note " that over 60 Lodges have not charged their members with the L.R.C. levy, thus weakening their position financially by drawing from Lodge funds. The apathy and want of interest by members in this Fund seems almost incredible. . . ."

Had the Executive known it, they were soon to meet not only apathy, but outright rebellion. Canning Town Lodge had already challenged at the D.M. the legality of the levy

imposed for L.R.C. purposes, although their delegate had
agreed that the question should be left in abeyance until a
decision had been given in a test case involving the South
Wales Miners' Federation. Contrary to this undertaking,
however, the Lodge later decided to launch an action against
the U.O.P.A. and publicised their intentions in *Reynolds News*.

The apparent situation in 1905 was described by the E.C.:
" It is legal to subscribe from the funds of the Association to
the promotion of Parliamentary Representation: it is not legal
to enforce a special levy for the purpose of promoting Parliamentary Representation unless provision is made in the rules
for the payment of such a levy. The view of the Chief Registrar, as we understand it, however, is that if it is legal to
subscribe to Parliamentary Representation it is unnecessary
to place it in the objects of the Association; while, if it is
illegal, the fact of its being in the objects as passed by the
Registrar would not make it legal." Two eminent lawyers,
consulted by the Executive Council, both advised that the
promotion of Parliamentary representation was within the
scope of a trade union's activity.

After some preliminary sparring between the E.C. and the
Lodge, the case was taken before the Manchester County
Court. The U.O.P.A. admitted that they had no rule authorising them to impose levies for the purpose of raising funds to
support the L.R.C., and the Judge was himself rather
bewildered by the insistence of the Lodge on an injunction, in
the face of the Association's admission. During the proceedings, Canning Town relented to the extent of offering to accept
a declaration by the Court that the U.O.P.A. should not make
any levy on the members of Canning Town Lodge " contrary
to the rules of the Society." Judgment was so given.

This last-minute compromise on the part of the com-
plainants thus nullified the significance of what might otherwise have been a critical case with repercussions among trade
unions generally. The acid test did not come until three years
later, when a Conservative secretary of a branch of the
Amalgamated Society of Railway Servants took legal action
to prevent the funds of the union from being used for political
ends. His challenge, like that of the Taff Vale Railway
Company's manager in 1901, went to the legal limit of the

House of Lords. The Law Lords, in what then became famous as the " Osborne Judgment," overturned previous judgments against Osborne and declared that it was illegal to make contributions to political parties from trade union funds. Another four years elapsed before this confusion was cleared away by the passing of the Trade Union (Amendment) Act, 1913.

As General Secretary of the U.O.P.A., Burns attended a conference of the Labour Party in February 1906 and complained about the circular issued by the Party in which Ramsay MacDonald had suggested that the Canning Town action might have been conducted more effectively if the Labour Party had been fully consulted in the first place. The circular did seem to imply that if the U.O.P.A. had left matters to the Labour Party the action might have precipitated a decision which was later to emerge from the Osborne Judgment. At the conference, MacDonald placated Burns by assuring him that the Party's Executive Committee would thoroughly investigate the whole problem in the light of prevailing legal opinion.

During these difficult times, unemployment was rising steadily and by the end of 1905 no less than 11.4 per cent of U.O.P.A. members were out of work. The dispute with the Scottish Society in Glasgow had ended in fiasco, with no credit at all to the Scots and scarcely more to the U.O.P.A., whose members finally capitulated and returned to work at a halfpenny an hour less but with guarantees that the working rules would otherwise remain unchanged for three years. The cost of this dispute must have been phenomenal.

Further attempts had been made during the year, this time on a regional basis, to establish conciliation machinery with the Master Builders' Association. When the proposed rules were submitted to U.O.P.A. members, however, they were firmly rejected. In fact, the only measure of encouragment during this period was drawn from the joint discussions between the Association, the Master Plumbers and the Royal Institute of British Architects; a number of local agreements were reached on the definition of plumbers' work. It is unlikely that these were much of a deterrent to the other unions with which the U.O.P.A. was in almost daily conflict:

G

and even here the promise of success soon evaporated. In his annual report for 1905 Burns declared: " Unfortunately the Institute (R.I.B.A.) have not seen fit to adopt our suggestion, I am afraid largely on account of the attitude of the employers at the interview, and I cannot help thinking that could we have foreseen the attitude the employers were going to take up and met the Institute ourselves, our efforts would have met with a greater degree of success than in simply being complimented on the interest we took in education and apprenticeship in our trade." Nothing in the 1905 garden was lovely.

A crude assessment of the Union's fortunes at this time can be made from the financial returns. Expenditure for 1905, at more than £43,000, exceeded total income by almost £14,000 and contributions by almost £16,000. Strike benefit alone amounted to £14,000 in the year.

The flickering illusion of plumbing trade unity was abruptly blacked out in 1906 when the National Association of Master Plumbers, having altered its title to " The Institute of Plumbers " and adopted new articles of association, invited the U.O.P.A. to support them in a new registration movement. For more than two decades, registration had been accepted as the sole preserve of the Worshipful Company and for this reason the U.O.P.A. Executive declined to co-operate—at least until the matter had been discussed at a Delegate Meeting. The problem of plumbing examinations and certification, however, did reach a satisfactory conclusion with an agreement between the Worshipful Company, the Master Plumbers, the City and Guilds and the U.O.P.A., which established an Advisory Committee to deal with such questions as the plumbing syllabus, certification, examiners and other matters connected with craft examinations.

The demarcation struggle over plumbing and heating work, hitherto confined to the operatives, now drew the masters' associations into the conflict. The National Association of Master Heating and Domestic Engineers entered the arena with a circular deploring " the attempts of the plumbers to secure a monopoly of the work of domestic hot water supply. The plumbers' claims," declared the masters, " are that all such work in any metal is plumbers' work only, and that it must not be undertaken by heating and domestic engineers. These claims have been successfully resisted, although in some cases the plumbers struck work, and caused serious loss and annoyance to all concerned." They concluded by quoting a joint resolution agreed between their Association and the Master Plumbers, stipulating that "all lead work be considered plumbers' work, but that a neutral line be taken as regards all iron, brass, copper, or other metal work, which may be executed by engineers or plumbers." At the same time they published a letter from the R.I.B.A. which said, in effect, that the dispute over hot water work was really no affair of the Institute, which was concerned only "with the improvement and efficiency of craftsmanship." The U.O.P.A. must have felt that every man's hand was against them.

Not even the members themselves were co-operative. The E.C. had drafted an amendment to rule to allow the Association to enforce levies for the purpose of "meeting any case of emergency; paying affiliation fees to any recognised body . . . for returning (Labour) members to Parliament . . ." etc., provided that such levies were first approved by a vote of the members. The amendment was turned down by a majority of nearly two to one. So, too, was a suggestion that the U.O.P.A. should promote their own Parliamentary candidate.

In September 1906, the first "four-party" meeting took place in the Midland Hotel, Birmingham, between representatives of the U.O.P.A. (Burns, Edmiston and E.C. member W. H. Hamilton), the Master Plumbers, Heating Engineering Employers and operatives. After some severe preliminary interrogation it was established that the operative heating engineers represented three small societies operating in London, Liverpool and Birmingham. The ensuing discussion was a heated one, but the results were negligible. Certainly no positive move was made by any party towards hammering out a common policy as the basis for a workable demarcation agreement. That the U.O.P.A. leaders had no intention of abandoning their traditional stand on "plumbers' work" was made quite clear later in the month, when Burns used the local Press to reply at great length to a letter from the architect for Leigh Infirmary which had recently been the centre of a bitter dispute over the allocation of hot water services. Burns, while admitting the architect's right to allocate the several classes of work to be done, argued that " plumbers formerly jointed (copper) pipes in the same way that lead pipes are jointed, then we experienced no difficulty; but when we commenced to screw the pipes then the handy labourer and others who have since generated into pipe-fitters and so-called " heating engineers " were brought into existence at wages of from 4½d. to 7d. per hour. Our claim is that all pipes in all metals conveying water for domestic or sanitary purposes shall be done by plumbers; heating may be done by plumbers or others, and much difficulty will be avoided by those in authority declaring that plumbers must be employed on such domestic or sanitary work."

The Plumbers moved into London for the first time in 1907 and set up headquarters at 181, Clapham Road, Stockwell. In accordance with the revised rule the Executive Council were drawn from members of Lodges within a 12-mile radius. Among the members of the first London E.C. were Fred Wyatt (Fulham), F. Barter (Battersea), F. Randall (London No. 1) and J. R. Beeston (West Central), who later became full-time District Secretary for the London area.

It was not a propitious time for a new team to take office. Craft warfare was still widespread; the A.S.E. had told the U.O.P.A. that their rules were being altered from December 1907 to allow the admission of ship plumbers; more than 8 per cent of the Association's members were out of work; and a suggestion by the Master Plumbers that the crucial issue of hot-water fitting should be referred to arbitration was flatly rejected by the E.C.

Returns were now being published monthly and included an " open column " in which any member was free to express his views and opinions. Most of the early correspondence was concerned with the Canning Town case and the wider issue of the political levy. Other correspondents dealt at length with the conflict between plumbers and other trades.

At this time there appears to have been a growing tendency for Lodges to co-operate on regional bases, thus creating quite spontaneously a structure now embodied in the Union's machinery. In their report for 1907 the Union's auditors felt it necessary, in rather supercilious terms, " to call the attention of members to the fact that in some districts they appear to have what they style ' District Councils,' for which charges are made on the funds of the Association. We are not aware of the functions of these Councils or what benefit the Association as a whole derives from their existence, and we are agreed that not being authorised by Rule, any further expenditure in connection with such Councils will be surcharged to the Lodge or Lodges to be repaid by levy."

It is odd to find the auditors (who, after all, were themselves members of the U.O.P.A.) feigning innocence of a situation that must have existed in various regions for many years. Earlier in 1907, for example, the returns contained a report of a presentation to John H. Edmiston on his retirement as secretary " after fourteen years of gratuitous service to the Manchester District Council, i.e., a body of delegates representing branches of the U.O.P.A. within a radius of 20 miles of Manchester, and who meet together for the purpose of discussing and remedying by conciliatory means local grievances and generally interesting themselves in all organisation and association work. . . ." Moreover, for several years the London Lodges had enjoyed the privilege of representation on the " London Management Committee " which was similar in constitution and functions to the District Committee of today. The obvious answer to this enigma is that the establishment of " these Councils " was quite acceptable to the U.O.P.A. management so long as Association funds were not involved.

In his report for the same year, Burns mentioned the inquiry held by the E.C. into the financial position of the U.O.P.A. This revealed that the Association's funds had steadily decreased over the three preceding years; the decline was attributed mainly to the unexpectedly high level of out-of-work benefit payments and the increase in superannuation benefit claims. The Executive recommended an age limit of 50 for the latter and reductions in the scale of payments, with a separate additional contribution of 2d. a week for those members qualifying. There were other suggestions for

tightening up on benefit payments and Lodge management
expenses. Total expenditure at this period was running at
55s. 2½d. per member per annum; out-of-work benefit
accounted for 15s. 7d. and sickness benefit for 10s. 5d. Strike
benefit, at 3s. 2d. a head, was comparatively low. The
imbalance between expenditure on trade protection and
advancement on the one hand and friendly society benefits on
the other had again moved markedly in favour of the latter,
and was a severe handicap to the Association's potential activities in the industrial field.

Fresh overtures, this time from the Heating Engineering
Employers, to secure the reference of the conflict over heating
work to arbitration under the Board of Trade's Labour
Department, met with a frigid response from the Plumbers.
The Ironmonger (no friend of the U.O.P.A.) reported in April
1908 that " the aggressive campaign by which the operative
plumbers hope to deprive the domestic engineer of his right
to fitting and fixing hot-water supply services in hard metals
has been made possible by the lack of efficient organisation
among the operative domestic engineers. This plumbers'
question and other matters affecting the operative domestic
engineers will be dealt with in future, we hope, in an effective
and vigorous manner by a new union, to be known as the
National Union of Operative Heating and Domestic
Engineers, which amalgamates three existing societies, viz.:
The United Fitters' and Smiths' Society, Birmingham; The
Amalgamated Society of Whitesmiths and Domestic
Engineers, Liverpool; and the Hot-Water and Steam
Engineers' Society, Birmingham, all of which have numerous
branches in different towns. . . . A joint conference has been
arranged to sit at Nottingham in Easter week, when the new
union will be launched."

The Plumbers' sins of omission, in spite of twenty years'
hammering by Cherry and Burns, had finally come home to
roost.

CHAPTER VI

THE LOWEST EBB

THE fortunes of the United Operative Plumbers' Association of Great Britain and Ireland were surely moving towards their nadir when even the spirit of brotherhood, which so dramatically characterised the early trade unions, was shown in 1908 to be almost extinct. A long dispute on Tyneside had resulted in the lock-out of hundreds of U.O.P.A. members. The prospect of an early settlement was remote. It was the unhappy task of the E.C. to publicly " regret the apathy of the members, as shown by the result of the vote taken for and against a levy of 6d. per member per week for the purpose of meeting the extraordinary expenditure incurred by our brethren on the N.E. Coast being locked-out through the strike of other trades. The members having failed to realise the heavy financial responsibility cast upon the Association through the above-mentioned cause, and the further strain thrown upon our already weakened resources by the declaration of a general lock-out of the shipbuilding trades, together with the depression of trade in general, leaves the E.C. with no alternative but to make a call for funds, in accordance with General Rule, of 6s. 6d. per equalised member for the previous quarter."

In 1908 during the summer months, usually favourable to building workers' employment, unemployment among members of the U.O.P.A. reached the staggering peak of 13.24 per cent of the total membership. The Tyneside lock-out partly accounted for this burden, but Lodge returns indicated that trade was very bad in general. Towards the end of the year, a famous name appeared in the annals of the Association: the Right Hon. Winston Churchill. At that time President of the Board of Trade, he had suggested in a speech at Dundee that there should be a Department of State charged with the responsibility of counterbalancing fluctuations in trade and the labour market, so that recurring economic slumps and resultant heavy unemployment could be banished for all time. He also complained about the use of " boy labour " and the growing evil of casual labour. By and large the U.O.P.A.

were sympathetic towards Churchill's proposed remedies for unemployment, although they asked pointedly: " Is Mr. Churchill, as President of the Board of Trade, prepared to move the Government to enforce these views, and require qualification of workmen to be recognised in Government contracts and public works? In short, let him recognise that trade unions collectively represent the barrier which practically protects craftsmanship against debasement by that kind of commercialism which looks to profit, irrespective of the quality of work."

In a report on education and apprenticeship in the plumbing trade, Burns was not so sympathetic towards a practice he had noticed " in some quarters for Masters to permit their apprentices to leave work in order to attend classes during the day. Such an arrangement does not seem to me at all practicable as a general system. During apprenticeship I consider that the practice of the trade in the workshop should be supplemented and strengthened by educational training of a practical kind in the technical classes. It is found that lads can attend evening instruction without prejudice to their health or well-being." Burns was, however, in favour of another new development in this field: pre-apprenticeship training. " At fourteen, the lad should proceed to the ' Pre-Apprenticeship ' School and continue there until he is sixteen. . . ."

At the end of the year, registration stirred again from its almost prostrate position with the inauguration by the Worshipful Company of a General Council for the National Registration of Plumbers, to whom the Plumbers' Company handed over the management and administration of the movement. A full report on these developments, appearing in a trade journal (possibly *The Ironmonger,* judging by the line of approach), was followed by an editorial comment: " It will be gathered from the foregoing report that the Worshipful Company of Plumbers are on the warpath again. Baffled in their endeavours to induce Parliament to grant them the monopoly rights they so much desire, they have come to the conclusion, apparently, that as they have not succeeded alone, it would be a good plan to try what concerted action will do. Accordingly, while retaining to themselves the main objects for which they are striving—namely, registration, and inferentially the collecting of annual fees, and the power to suspend and prosecute offenders—they have persuaded the Royal Institute of British Architects, the Association of Water Engineers, and several other quite eminent but at the same time, so far as this work is concerned, self-appointed bodies, to nominate certain of their members to join hands with them in the work of protecting the public, and incidentally creating a monopoly in a certain craft. The new movement will need to be watched by all who are interested in maintaining the right of any man to engage in any work he is qualified to perform irrespective of registration or, indeed, of any extraneous support. The new cry may be proclaimed by the voice of Jacob, but the hand to take and the fingers that will tighten on the unwary are unmistakably those of Esau." Strong stuff, this—yet it evoked no comment from the U.O.P.A. leaders.

The first hint of the imminent crisis that was to strain the unity of plumbers almost to breaking point appeared in the " Open Column " in March 1909. Since the issue of the E.C.'s report on the finances of the Association, followed by the report of an Actuary on the U.O.P.A. superannuation benefit, there had been an ominous absence of comment of any kind. But one member in Glasgow Govan Lodge, at least, had been doing some hard thinking. In his published letter, accompanied by some impressive financial tables, he asked the E.C. a number of pertinent questions. " Having held the inquiry and published the results, what do they desire members to do ' twixt this and the next D.M.? ' What steps are being taken by the E.C. with the 106 Lodges not complying with rule? If a real effort had been made by these Lodges to meet their liabilities, all the E.C.'s drastic proposals would never have seen the light of day."

Bro. Munro then referred to the financial returns of 12 Lodges, having a total of 1,330 members, who in 1907 were in debt to the U.O.P.A. to the tune of nearly £1,500. " I would earnestly ask my fellow members," he concluded, " to

look the facts in the face, and to speak out if they wish to
retain our Association in a useful and healthy condition."

The fact that had the ugliest face was the loss of more than
£21,500 in the Association's total funds during the period 1904-
1908. Of the balance at the end of 1904, over half had
disappeared.

With the issue of the Auditor's Report for 1908, the E.C.
were stung into action. The July returns for 1909 contained
a grave warning: " Our G.S. states that at our present rate
of expenditure we cannot, with the available funds at the
General Office, go on longer than two years. Can we allow
the present state of things to go on until we have lost all the
funds and then announce we are insolvent? Our answer is
NO, and we are confident there is not a member amongst us
who fears to know the truth before it is too late to save the
Association from ruin." As a temporary expedient the E.C.
proposed that payment of out-of-work benefit be suspended
at the end of the September quarter until the financial situation
justified a resumption. Ironically, as it happened, they also
made specific mention of defalcations by four Lodge Officers,
involving a total sum of about £250. " Unfortunately,"
declared the E.C., " there have been some black sheep amongst
the members who have held office. . . ." Only a few weeks
later they were to discover that the shepherd was the same
colour.

The writing was on the wall in the August open column.
John H. Edmiston (Manchester No. 2) complained of delays
in the issue of annual and quarterly reports and lack of
attention to important matters sent to General Office. " It
is quite time," he said, " somebody began to bestir themselves
at headquarters where there appears to be something radically
wrong, and which the sooner is put right the better, as there
are those who hold the Association too sacred to allow things
to continue as they are doing, and are prepared if needs be
to advocate a D.M. so as to put things on a proper footing
and the government in the hands of either person or persons
who will show the necessary amount of interest in the
Association and its members." Edmiston's letter was the
signal for a spate of correspondence from other members,
indicating that anxiety was sharpening in many quarters.

The fuse was finally lit quite involuntarily by the Wallsend Lodge Secretary, Bro. Joseph Blench, who had noticed in the March quarterly returns that £30 had been entered against Wallsend under the item " Cash sent to Lodges." He wrote to Burns to draw his attention to an error : the amount should have been £20. Burns disagreed. Bro. Blench then wrote to the Association's Treasurer, Bro. Fred Wyatt, who consulted the E.C. President and Vice-President. At one of the special E.C. meetings held in late August and early September, Bro. Blench was able to satisfy the E.C. completely that his assertion was correct.

With quickening dismay, the E.C. were forced to accept the appalling probability that the Association's leader was dishonest. At first, Burns feigned complete innocence; then he attempted to put the blame on an office boy who he alleged had " lost " some letters containing cheques; ultimately, confronted with other discrepancies between the printed returns and cash requisitions from Lodges, and with falsified receipts, he signed a confession admitting the misappropriation of about £70. The E.C. were human enough to ask him to resign. At the same time, however, they asked the members to decide whether or not Burns should be prosecuted—as, indeed, he was when it was later discovered that he had also helped himself to some £300 from a total of £580 collected by levy for the future support of the Labour Party. Burns pleaded guilty and was sentenced to eight months' imprisonment.

This unsavoury episode, which did not end with the sentencing of Burns, marked the lowest point in the fortunes of the U.O.P.A. Coming as it did at the peak of the worst financial crisis ever experienced by the Association, it must have been a cruel blow for the E.C. in particular and the members in general, who had regarded their General Secretary as the loyal servant of the U.O.P.A. and the custodian of its very slender resources.

Twenty-two candidates presented themselves to the membership in the first ballot to elect a new General Secretary. Among them were some familiar names: Fred Wyatt of Fulham, Lachlan MacDonald, John H. Edmiston and W. C. Walsh of Dublin. Eventually the contest was resolved into a straight fight between MacDonald and Edmiston (who, it will be remembered, had acted as temporary G.S. after Cherry's death). In a close finish, Edmiston was the victor by just over 300 votes in a poll of 4,500, and commenced his duties in March 1910.

In a generous tribute in the monthly report, Lachlan MacDonald appealed to the members to give their new leader their full confidence and support. "No man, however able he may be, can hope to achieve great things on our behalf if he does not feel that he has the whole-hearted confidence of those on whose behalf he is working. I do not ask you to trust him blindly. Criticise his actions if you choose, but avoid captious criticism, which is the essence of jealousy."

The Auditors' Report for 1909 spoke of the "experience unparalleled in its history" which had brought chaos to the Association's administration. They presented a full account of the verifiable deficiencies for which Burns had been responsible, but also hinted at further irregularities which could not positively be attributed to him. The incident was clearly having one beneficial effect in underlining the need for much closer and more frequent scrutiny of accounts, not only at G.O. but throughout the whole of the Association.

The report revealed that the financial outlook was brighter, although not rosy. In 1908 the U.O.P.A. lost nearly £7,000: in 1909 the loss was no more than £800. "Members must not think we are bankrupt," wrote the G.M.P., J. R. Beeston, "but it is not politic to wait until our funds are entirely depleted before taking action to put our house in order." He suggested that the next Delegate Meeting—only two years distant—should have firm proposals for putting the U.O.P.A. in the clear. Either an increase in contributions or a reduction in benefits (particularly superannuation and out-of-work) was felt to be inescapable. In ten years, superannuation payments had risen from £700 to £3,000 a year, while the Association had paid out £52,000 in out-of-work benefit over six years.

The deaths of 98 members were reported to G.O. during

1909 and it is interesting to note from the record that the average age at death was 46.

An important Parliamentary development of this period, to which the U.O.P.A. did full justice by publishing the whole Commons debate, was the amendment of the Fair Wages Clause in Government contracts. The Clause was first introduced in 1891 because of the evils resulting from unbridled competition by contractors for Governmental work. Previously, however, it had dealt only with wages: the new Resolution covered hours and conditions of work as well. The opening paragraph read: " The Fair Wages Clause in Government contracts should be so amended as to provide that the contractor shall, under penalty, pay to all workmen in his employ not less than the minimum standard rate of wages recognised by trade societies in the district where such men are employed, and shall observe the recognised hours and proper conditions of labour."

Although the years leading up to the first European holocaust are sometimes recalled with nostalgia as the " good old days," they were in reality years of violent industrial upheaval. Indeed in *Magnificent Journey* Francis Williams christens them the " Years of Violence " and points out that " there was hardly an industry in the country that was not torn by conflict at some time in the years from 1910 to 1914." According to official figures, 170,000 workers were involved in disputes in 1909; by 1911 the number had risen to more than 830,000 and reached nearly $1\frac{1}{4}$ million by 1912. Working days lost by strikes and lockouts in 1901 were calculated at 2,800,000; in 1912 the number was nearly 41 million. " All over Britain," says Francis Williams, " employers and workers alike seemed determined to turn their backs on negotiation and conciliation and give rein to their deepseated hostility in a series of industrial disputes that at times threatened to engulf the entire country in a vast social upheaval."

A lock-out of boilermakers in the shipbuilding industry in the latter half of 1910 had repercussions among ship plumbers and affected the Association's funds " to the extent of about £400 per week." Unemployment among U.O.P.A. members began to rise again and by November had reached the level of 12¼ per cent of membership. At the end of the year a vote of the members was taken to decide the venue of the forthcoming Delegate Meeting; London was chosen by a substantial majority.

At this time, too, there were regrettable echoes of the Burns affair, resulting in the resignation of the Assistant General Secretary, Tom Cherry, who was discovered by the Auditors to have been guilty of similar misdemeanours (though to a lesser degree) as his former chief. Twenty-seven members offered themselves for the vacancy, but the result of the first ballot made the need for a second ballot no more than a formality. Lachlan MacDonald of Glasgow, unsuccessful contender in the G.S. election a year earlier, polled over 1,100 votes against 560 votes of his nearest rival (Andrew Boyd, of Barrow). He duly secured a decisive majority on the next ballot and took office at the end of March 1911.

Early that year new moves were made to re-unite the U.O.P.A. with the Scottish Association. At a joint meeting in Manchester attended by five E.C. members from each body there was considerable common ground on the principle of amalgamation, although in finality no positive agreement emerged. The Scots wanted three things: local autonomy, abolition of out-of-work benefit, and a gradual increase in contributions for Scottish members until uniformity was reached with existing U.O.P.A. contributions. Later on they accepted compromise proposals on out-of-work benefit. John Edmiston concluded his report on the conference by remarking that " there appears to be a very strong feeling amongst members of both Associations that great benefit would accrue generally by a unity of forces."

A voice was raised in the " open column " in April 1911 that was later to become familiar and respected throughout the Association. The subject was domestic hot-water work. " The only way I can see for us to keep a hold on this work " the correspondent wrote, " is to alter the Rules of our Association so as to allow us to admit pipefitters. This I know will not find favour with some members, but I only ask them to look ahead a little. At present these pipefitters are organising, and have a National Organisation. Now the wisest plan for us is to alter our Rules, approach these people, and arrange

to take them before they build up a strong rival organisation
to our own. The cry on all hands is that there are too many
trade unions and too few trade unionists, a fact there is no
disputing. Our object should be to get these men into our
Association, and so get command of the heating and domestic
hot water work, and then set about to raise the standard of
pay for this work up to our own. Then in time it would
follow that the whole would be recognised as one trade."
The writer had clearly studied the sermons of Cherry. His
name was George H. Harris.

The 1911 Delegate Meeting was held in the Wirtemberg
Hall at Clapham. The business of dealing with amendments
to rules was not reached until the sixth day, when two early
decisions illustrated the contradictory and confused attitudes
still prevailing among organised plumbers on the age-old
question of U.O.P.A. membership. The meeting recorded
a half-hearted " no " to the proposition that " we shall admit
others than plumbers to our Association." Voting was 576
to 485. Next day, however, the Association's title was
amended to " The United Operative Plumbers' and Domestic
Engineers' Association of Great Britain and Ireland." The
latter decision can hardly have been received with enthusiasm
by those who had supported the former. During the remaining six days, delegates struggled through the hundreds of
proposed alterations until, as the report concludes, " the meeting terminated by singing heartily and lustily the Scottish
benediction ' Auld Lang Syne ' accompanied at the close
with three British cheers."
In an appendix to the report, the S.O.C. voiced their
dissatisfaction with the fact that many delegates had left the
D.M. long before the " Scottish benediction "—even at the
end of the first week. " We think some means should be
devised whereby the business of the D.M. could be curtailed,
as we feel sure that the Association cannot bear the strain of
the expense." Certainly Delegate Meetings were costly affairs
and the net result hardly justified the severe burden placed on
the Association's funds. Apart from a modified set of rules,

by no means revolutionary in themselves, the 1911 D.M. had appointed a special committee to examine the new State Insurance Scheme in relation to U.O.P.A. benefits and had convened two special conferences during the period of the D.M. itself. One of these dealt with demarcation and other matters affecting members in ship plumbing, while the other concerned " the edification and better organisation of members engaged in Chemical Works." They were innovations, to be sure, and laid the basis for the special conferences held occasionally in more recent times for the benefit of specialised sections of the Union's membership such as roofing felt workers, shipping members, gas industry members and so on. Nevertheless, the crucial function of any Delegate Meeting was the degree of re-direction and guidance imparted to the future affairs of the Association by the act of changing its rules. It must be recognised that in the exercise of this function the Delegate Meetings of old were extremely cautious and the evolution of the present General Rules has been a slow and expensive affair.

It would seem from the records that the two most important decisions to emerge in 1911 were the raising of contributions to 1s. 3d. a week and the incorporation of direct Labour Representation as one of the objects of the Association.

In the industrial field, support was growing for a suggestion that the Engineering and Shipbuilding Trades Federation should deal with " all conditions of employment and have a common financial liability in respect to all trade movements." The Federation appealed to affiliated unions to sound out the feelings of the members. The question was accordingly submitted to a Lodge vote of U.O.P.A. members in September 1911 and by a decisive majority of nearly seven to one they indicated their support for common action by the Federation on behalf of all affiliates.

By this time, as a result of an earlier Lodge vote, Union headquarters had been removed from London to Newcastle, with G.O. at 82, Osborne Road and an entirely new Executive Council including Bro. J. Blench (Wallsend), S. Sigsworth (South Shields—later a member of the first full-time E.C.) and W. J. Glover (Newcastle, subsequently full-time D.S. for the North-East Coast District).

MANCHESTER EXECUTIVE COUNCIL, 1904

H. Sharp, E. E. Collicutt, T. H. Cherry (A.G.S.), G. Cresswell, F. Brindley, J. Forrest, J. Simpson,
J. H. Edmiston, W. Cubin, G. McPherson
E. E. Burns (G.S.), H. Hamilton (G.M.P.), W. L. Maddocks

EXECUTIVE COUNCIL AND GENERAL OFFICERS, 1921

Lachlan MacDonald (front, left) and his colleagues on the steps of 15, Abbeville Road

The year 1912 began promisingly. "Not only does the prospective of our members look brighter," remarked the E.C., " but there are decided indications that our Association is also on the upward path; we are confident that with sustained efforts the prestige of our Association as one of the leading Associations in the United Kingdom will be maintained." The black years of 1904-1909, though not forgotten, were already gathering the patina of history. Unemployment was running at a mere $4\frac{1}{2}$ per cent of membership, and increasing recognition by Parliament of the need for measures to alleviate distress and hardship among the working population was moving towards its pre-war climax with the passing of the first Insurance Act, providing for statutory contributions and benefits for sickness and unemployment, which was the foundation of modern National Insurance legislation.

In fact, state insurance dominated the affairs of the U.O.P.A. in particular and figured largely in British trade unionism generally during 1912, since the Act made provision for unions with more than 5,000 members to become " Approved Societies " for the purpose of administering benefits. There was consequent upheaval in the internal systems of the trade unions, if only because of the extra paper work involved and the need for separate financial records to be maintained.

Lachlan MacDonald, the A.G.S., made a special study of the new Act and its relation to U.O.P.A. contributions and benefits. In March he presented a paper to the E.C. which outlined the main provisions of the Act, its implications and deficiencies as he saw them, and the demands it would make on the Union's administration. He did more than this: he put forward detailed proposals for revising the U.O.P.A.'s contributions and benefits to make allowance for the statutory insurance contributions and varying degrees of eligibility for benefit under the State scheme. He was the architect of the Tables of contributions and benefits as we now know them.

It was most unfortunate for the Plumbers that in the light of these important national developments the echoes of " three British cheers " from the 1911 D.M. had scarcely died away than the need arose for a further meeting. The need, however, was not immediately apparent to the E.C. In May

H

they convened a joint meeting of the full E.C. and the Special
Committee set up in 1911 to study the insurance problem.
After some strong objections by members of the Special Committee to the intervention of the E.C. had been overcome,
the meeting got down to business. Six days were spent on
producing revised General Rules, on the basis laid down by
Lachlan MacDonald, to conform to the requirements of the
Insurance Act and to ensure that the U.O.P.A. would be
accepted as an Approved Society.

Once again, the E.C. acted rather prematurely and found
themselves faced with the demand for a Delegate Meeting.
This time the call came not from the members but from the
Health Insurance Commissioners, who declared quite
adamantly that alterations to U.O.P.A. rules made by the
Special Committee acting jointly with the E.C. were not
substantiated unless approved by a D.M. With unseemly
haste the twelfth Delegate Meeting was duly arranged at the
Co-op Hall, Darn Crook, Newcastle, at the end of August.

Delegates may have been befuddled by the chaotic rapidity
of events, but this did not deter them from launching two
early " haymakers " at the top brass. First target was the
Special Committee, censured " for having exceeded their duties
by framing rules without first submitting them to the country
for their votes, also for having dealt with rules for which
they had received no mandate from the last D.M." Then
came a strong protest " against the action of the E.C. in claiming to take part in the deliberations of the Special Committee."
This concluded the first day's business.

For three more days the D.M. laboured, adding the
semblance of a democratic facade—in the form of minor
amendments to the Tables of Contributions and Benefits—
to what in effect was a " rubber stamp " assembly demanded
by law. The model rules were endorsed. This was all to
the good, since they had already been approved by the
Insurance Commissioners more than a month earlier.

The United Association of Operative Plumbers (and
Domestic Engineers) thus became an Approved Society in
common with many other unions for the purpose of
administering State Insurance benefits. This new function,
which added considerably to the burden of work at G.O., was

to endure for nearly 35 years until the responsibilities were finally vested in the State under the National Insurance Act of 1946.

Even without the birth of national insurance, 1912 would have been a busy year for the Association. There was a revival of the movement for " one union for the building industry " following the adoption at the 1911 Congress of the T.U.C. of a resolution from the Bricklayers' Society in favour of industrial unionism. The T.U.C. Parliamentary Committee arranged a conference of building trade union representatives and the outlines of a scheme to establish " The Amalgamated Building Workers' Union " were approved. The scheme was then referred to individual unions for endorsement by the members.

Although the Plumbers' E.C. had given qualified support to the initial proposals, they made it quite clear that " we do *not* intend to lose our individuality as an organisation or even to become merged into one common union with *one* fund. What we *do* suggest is that the time of sectional disputes has passed, and that an amalgamation of *interests,* with each organisation bearing its share, for offensive and defensive purposes, has now become a necessity." In short, the E.C. wanted federation, not integration.

So, too, did most of the building unions. When the voting figures were published it was clear that the principle was generally accepted, but the practice, involving loss of identity, was another kettle of fish. Raymond Postgate comments that the voting figures showed that " though the industrial unionists had secured a majority in every trade, they had failed to move the dead weight of ' insurance members.' Those who had been merely forced to pay lip service to amalgamation through fear of an enormous rank-and-file vote were encouraged by the figures to break away. The A.S.C.J. (Carpenters and Joiners) Executive decided that it would take no further votes on amalgamation, on the ground that it preferred federation, and the defection of so important and wealthy a union was a very severe blow indeed."

The U.O.P.A. vote yielded a return of approximately one-sixth of the total membership, with a majority in favour of amalgamation. In later ballots, however, members joined forces with the E.C. and decisively rejected the detailed proposals for the establishment of the Building Workers' Union.

Another revival in 1912 took the form of a new campaign for the introduction of an eight-hour working day. This also sprang from a T.U.C. resolution. The campaign was inaugurated in Newcastle with a massive procession of trade unionists and Labour leaders, followed by speeches from three separate platforms: at one of these Lachlan MacDonald presided, with support from E.C. member T. McKenna and Labour M.P., Will Thorne. An important landmark in industrial relations in the shipbuilding industry was the approval of the 1912 Demarcation Agreement, which was to remain the industry's main arbitration instrument for many years to come.

Domestically the U.O.P.A. made good progress in that year. Membership rose by over 600 and funds increased by about £8,000. It was the last occasion on which the Association accounts were audited by members elected to perform that duty. From 1913 the responsibility was passed over to Chartered Accountants (on a decision of the Delegate Meeting) partly, no doubt, in the interests of security and partly because of the magnitude the task had reached with the advent of National Insurance and the growing complexity of the Association's financial affairs.

As might have been expected, the first Annual Report by the professionals contained some pungent remarks on the financial methods, practices and returns of U.O.P.A. Lodge Secretaries and the book-keeping systems operating at all levels. It is to the credit of the Newcastle Executive Council that they took heed of the experts' advice and held a special meeting in 1914 to devise ways and means of implementing the Accountants' detailed suggestions.

Quite unobtrusively the Association's structure was undergoing an important change. At the 1911 D.M., the Lodge Committee rule had been extended to give official recognition to District Committees, which, as we have seen, had operated in certain regions for many years. But this was by no means a token recognition of a *fait accompli*. The E.C. prepared a schedule of Lodges, grouped according to the 20-mile-radius requirement of the rule, which could form their own District Committees with effect from September 1913. What is more, after some preliminary quibbling on the interpretation of the financial aspects of the rule, they notified members a year later that " for the better and more efficient working of the District Committees, the E.C. have decided that all expenses, except those incurred for organising purposes, shall be a direct charge to the Equalisation Account."

The opening words of the rule, " A District Committee of lodges within a twenty-mile radius shall be appointed " had the peculiar and unintentional result of excluding certain large Lodges from forming or participating in a District Committee from the beginning. Among the " outcasts " were four Lodges which today are regional centres of the Union: Aberdeen, Belfast, Edinburgh and Cambridge. Giving the list of excluded Lodges, the E.C. remarked: " The obvious remedy is undoubtedly in their hands, and wherever possible they should endeavour to organise the opening of a new lodge. The Executive Council will be only too pleased to encourage efforts in that direction."

By 1913 the Plumbers' bitterest rivals were organised into a national association, later to become the Heating and Domestic Engineers' Union. The warnings of George Cherry were now seen in the ultimate form. Even the U.O.P.A. members themselves had to face the unpalatable fact, and although their decision was suggestive of " locking the stable door after the horse has bolted," they finally threw in the towel and accepted the E.C.'s proposal to seek discussions on amlagamation with the H.E.U. and to accept heating engineers and pipefitters into membership of the U.O.P.A. The decision was not made lightly; in a total vote of 3,132 the majority barcly exceeded 800. Nevertheless, after thirty years of resistance to persuasion the step had been taken and they had made the supreme sacrifice on the altar of progress. The tragedy was that it had been so long delayed.

Authority from the members was also sought and obtained by the E.C. to participate in a conference convened by the Labour Department of the Board of Trade for the purpose of arbitrating on the issue of domestic hot water supplies. In January 1914, however, the E.C. declared: " It is not our intention to agree to arbitration on the question, for the simple reason that we have nothing to arbitrate upon. Lodges should therefore refuse temporary settlements unless the work in dispute is given to the plumbers."

Tentative approaches by the E.C. to the rival organisation had already foundered. The Executive had informed members in September 1913, rather sadly, that they had " made certain suggestions to them as a basis . . . whereby the two Associations could be merged into one, and by this means bring to an end the strife which keeps breaking out by reason of repeated encroachments upon the work of the Plumber. Your E.C. regret to announce that their efforts have been futile, the E.C. of the Heating Engineers having signified their inability to recommend their members to consider the matter, but instead they suggest we should have a working agreement only, on the line that they should continue to do the work in dispute. This your E.C. cannot consent to. We have often had applications from hot water fitters to join our Association, but having in view the possibility of amalgamation have refused to accept them. The time has now arrived when we should no longer refuse these men into membership. Let there be no parley in this matter, but each member show a determination that the Plumbing Trade must be under the control of the Plumbers."

The bitter industrial strife that had characterised the previous years had abated considerably by 1913. Among the encouraging features of that year was the passing of the Trade Union Act which finally restored to trade unions the political freedom they had been denied by the Osborne Judgment. For the U.O.P.A., one of the most heartening developments was an increase in membership of more than 1,200.

But these were flashes of light in a gathering darkness. Although an uneasy peace extended throughout British industry, there was conflict of the most savage kind in Ireland, where Dublin strikers and their families were subjected to brutal and humiliating attacks by the Royal Irish Constabulary and the Dublin police. From the organising efforts of James Connolly grew the Irish Citizens' Army, originally formed for the defence of the workers against the excesses of the police, but later to the developed into a disciplined fighting force that made history in 1916.

Back on this side of the Irish Sea more trouble was brewing. A series of strikes occurred late in 1913 among London building workers over the issue of non-unionism. Suddenly the London Master Builders sprang into action and on 24th January, 1914, some thirty to forty thousand building operatives were locked out. They would not be re-employed unless they signed " the document," which on this occasion took the following form: " I agree, if employed by you, to peacefully work with my fellow employees (engaged either in your direct employment or in that of any sub-contractor) whether they are members of a trade society or not, and I agree that I will not quit your employment because any of your employees is or is not a member of any trade society; and I also agree that if I commit any breach of this agreement I will be subject to a fine of twenty shillings, and I agree that the amount of such fine may be deducted from any wages which may be due to me."

Raymond Postgate says : " The great conflict of 1914 bears a fantastic resemblance to the lock-outs of 1834, of 1859 and, to a certain extent, of 1872. It arose from an attempt by the operatives to secure an advantage. It ended unsuccessfully for the workers after the masons had broken away. It concentrated, while it was on, the whole attention of the trade union world."

The lock-out might have ended in April when the Master Builders, faced with determined resistence from the workers (including thousands of " nons "), withdrew the document under terms drawn up by the National Conciliation Board. Union Executives would have been satisfied with this; but the rank and file, among whom the influence of the militant London Building Industries Federation was very powerful, were resolved not to yield until some concession had been offered by the Masters on the original issue of non-unionism. The lock-out dragged on for eight months; resolution was eventually undermined by sectional settlements and crumbled beneath greater pressures that were bearing down on the whole nation on a scale never known before.

It was August 1914. An obscure European nobleman had been shot down in an even more obscure European town. What followed needs no narration here. The words of the A.G.S., Lachlan MacDonald, may be worth repeating as an indication of the immediate reactions of the trade unionist of the day. " Those wirepullers who are chiefly responsible for this international catastrophe are very ready to say that the strike is a most barbarous method of settling industrial disputes and we are bound to admit that we do not like it; but can anything more diabolical be invented than their way of settling international disputes? If half the money that is spent yearly in worship at the shrine of the war-gods was spent in propagating peace it would be impossible to conceive of a war such as has now commenced. What is the workers' share? A legacy of bereft mothers and children, of desolate homes, of abject misery. Do we all love war? If not, why do we tolerate it? Did I hear someone say politics? Yes, brother, it is politics, and so long as we are hoodwinked into believing that as trade unionists we should not take part in politics, so long will these things continue. Our very existence as an organisation is so interwoven with politics that if we don't soon take a hand in them we shall leave such a legacy to posterity that it shall be said of us 'twere ' better they had never lived '."

CHAPTER VII

"YOUR COUNTRY NEEDS YOU"

THERE is no place in these pages for more than a brief reference to the slaughter of British manhood which continued in France, Belgium and elsewhere for over four weary years. We can only concern ourselves with changes in the structure and fortunes of the U.O.P.A. which occurred during the first great international conflict of the twentieth century and which, to some extent, were the result of that conflict. It is always depressing to acknowledge the indisputable fact that war creates many beneficial by-products, stimulating and accelerating social changes which, in peacetime, can be the subject of protracted and often fruitless efforts.

The national emergency and the desperate need for munitions of war almost eliminated industrial strife in Britain. For the first time in the nation's history, "full employment" was more than just a Socialist's dream. Among U.O.P.A. members, for example, unemployment in relation to membership fell from 8.8 per cent in July 1914 to 2.0 per cent in 1915, 0.2 per cent in 1916 and 0.1 per cent (only 12 members) in February 1918.

The financial trend in the Association's affairs was even brighter. Total funds at the end of 1911 had been £22,726; by the end of 1915 they had soared to £52,083 and had nearly doubled again by December 1918, when they stood at £101,947 —equivalent to over £7 per member. There was also a steady increase in membership from 12,865 in 1914 to over 14,000 at the end of the war.

In a letter published in March 1915, great changes were foreshadowed—with almost prophetic accuracy—by a member of Cardiff Lodge, E. A. Lowe. Speaking of the difficulties in trying to man an organisation with part-time officials, he put forward a number of suggestions for the reformation of the Association's structure. Among them were the centralisation of G.O., abolition of the movable E.C., and the appointment of full-time District Secretaries. Bro. Lowe felt that the reorganisation of the U.O.P.A. on these lines would be far the best way of celebrating its " Jubilee " in 1915. As it happened, the Jubilee was never celebrated. It was crushed beneath the weight of world events.

By mid-1915, ten per cent of the Association's members were on active service with the Forces. The E.C. had already decided that such members would have their cards kept " clear " for the duration and would be reinstated at the end of hostilities. They also introduced a special levy to provide funeral benefit for the dependants of members killed on active service. Both decisions were endorsed by a Lodge vote.

The " Joint Reference Committee," forerunner of the National Joint Council for the Plumbing Industry, sent a letter to architects in 1915 in which reference was made to the repeated disputes over encroachments by other trades on plumbers' work. The Committee, consisting of representatives of the U.O.P.A. and the Master Plumbers, declared: " The signatories to this memorandum resent the attempts that this important part of their work should be diverted from its legitimate channel, and feel compelled to offer determined opposition to all such attempts. With great respect we suggest that the friction can be obviated by members of the Architectural Profession including this work in the Plumber's Bill of Quantities, where until recently it was to be found, in all circumstances and in all cases." This joint appeal by the plumbers brought a prompt retaliatory circular from the heating engineers, Masters and Operatives, which the E.C. decided to " treat with the contempt it deserves." Industrial peace seemed as remote to the U.O.P.A. at the end of 1915 as international peace.

Important issues were decided during 1916. According to rule it was again time to re-locate General Office; John Edmiston's term as General Secretary was nearly complete, and another Delegate Meeting was due in 1917. But the war dragged on. The Executive proposed that the D.M. should therefore be postponed; as before, there was some dissension in the ranks (particularly after the almost equal division of votes on the postponement) with the result that a compromise solution was found. The E.C. accepted, gracefully, a suggestion from Cardiff that " a joint Conference be held, composed of two members from each district along with the E.C., to take into consideration certain matters and submit their findings to the whole of the Association."

London challenged Newcastle in the final ballot for G.O. Commonsense won the day and U.O.P.A. headquarters (and the Executive Council) remained on Tyneside. Edmiston was re-elected by a comfortable majority. During the course of his election, however, a situation emerged which led to the introduction of a feature now familiar in the Union's election procedure. A Liverpool member was nominated in his absence and found, much to his surprise, that his name appeared on the ballot paper as a candidate. It was too late to take remedial action, and some votes were wasted. The E.C. decided that in all future elections the *written* consent must be given by any nominee for a full-time appointment.

Although the U.O.P.A. members, in common with other trade unionists, accepted broadly the industrial restrictions imposed during the war-time emergency, they dug their heels in firmly in 1917 when the Admiralty introduced a scheme for organising shipyard labour for the purpose of increasing production of naval and merchant vessels. With the excuse of the increasing U-boat menace they attempted to impose on all shipyard workers a scheme depending on the acceptance of piecework. This was anathema to the plumbers, who registered their determined opposition to P.B.R. and similar methods of wage calculation. Members were warned that if they violated this basic principle of the U.O.P.A. they were liable to a fine of 5s. a day.

During 1916, with nearly a sixth of the members serving their country, only £46 was paid out in strike benefit. There was a sudden demand for the revival of leadburning, the highly-skilled craft once prominent in the work of the plumber but which, over the years, had gradually fallen into neglect, largely because of the increasing use of other metals such as copper and zinc. The use of lead sheet for roof coverings was also diminishing and was to some extent being replaced by a new material known as " Ruberoid." Inevitably, disagreements arose between joiners, slaters and plumbers over the fixing of this material until, in March 1916, a Board of Conciliation in Liverpool declared that the work should be done by plumbers " in all cases where Ruberoid or similar material is substituted for the materials usually used by plumbers on roofs."

In the same year Lachlan MacDonald was taken seriously ill and entered hospital for a major operation. He was out of action for more than two years. In his absence the E.C. appointed the G.M.P., Harry Atkinson of Newcastle, as temporary A.G.S.

After a request from the Board of Trade that every possible step should be taken to end the conflict over domestic hot water supplies, the E.C. announced in June 1916 that conferences had taken place between the four parties involved (operatives and employers) and that a sub-committee had been appointed to draw up a scheme for submission to the various Associations. At a final conference in Birmingham, despite the absence of the " Operative Hot Water Engineers," approval was tentatively given to a scheme in which clear lines of demarcation were laid down and provisions made for settlement of disputes by a Conciliation Board consisting of two representatives from each of the four parties, with the Secretaries. " Taking all the circumstances into consideration," said the E.C., " we feel that the scheme will, if accepted, bring about at least an honourable peace. It must be remembered that the Hot Water Engineers are a growing body, and the longer the delay, the more powerful our opposition. The E.C. assure you that a genuine attempt has been made to bring to a conclusion a position which has been a constant source of annoyance and expense." Submitted to a Lodge vote, the scheme was endorsed : but it was never implemented. A few months later it was to be thrown out.

The special conference arranged in substitution for the postponed D.M. was held in April 1917 in the William Morris Club, Clayton Street, Newcastle. The agenda was limited to certain specific items, including the position of Forces members, the proposed agreement on hot water supplies, suggestions for a national plumbing apprenticeship scheme, and payment by results. The fact that the E.C. had presented a fixed " menu " did not deter the conference from authorising the S.O.C. to accept any other resolutions that delegates might wish to hand in. Because of this decision—unconventional though it was—the conference had a much more profound effect on the future of the Association than it otherwise would have done.

The proposed demarcation agreement was rejected. Instead, the E.C. were instructed to renew their efforts to achieve amalgamation with the rival union. There was wholehearted agreement " that payment by results cannot be applied to our trade with successful results and we strongly oppose any attempt of the Government to enforce such a system." Approval was given to the scheme compiled jointly by the E.C. and the Institute of Plumbers for the establishment of a " National Scheme for Technical Training and Apprenticeship in the Plumbing Trade for Great Britain and Ireland ": this was the inception of the Plumbing Trades National Apprenticeship Council, with its local and regional machinery.

Undoubtedly, these were important matters. But the decisions that would recast the shape of the U.O.P.A. had yet to be made. The rank and file's determination that drastic alterations to the structure of their Association were overdue became apparent in the suggestions contained in the first three of twenty additional resolutions handed to the S.O.C. Liverpool and Manchester, ever prominent in the Association's affairs, were in the forefront of the sponsors of a National Executive Council—a proposal which met with unanimous approval. The S.O.C., augmented by three other members and the two General Officers, were given the task of drawing up two alternative schemes for presentation to the members. The conference also accepted a new draft of the District Committee rule which would permit much greater regional activity and development than had formerly been possible. Quite clearly, great schemes were afoot.

Nevertheless, nothing substantial could be accomplished immediately. As the Executive rightly pointed out, the special conference had no power to alter the rules; and even if its recommendations were endorsed by a vote of members they could then only be submitted " as ground work for the next D.M."

The Great War period produced abnormal acceleration in

other movements within the trade union sphere which might otherwise have developed with far less speed. In 1914, federation at national level among the building unions seemed as distant as it had been after the collapse of Robert Owen's " Grand National Consolidated " nearly eighty years earlier. It is true that a " syndicalist " organisation had arisen in 1914 with the title " Building Workers' Industrial Union," but this organisation aroused such antagonism among leaders of the established craft unions that they in turn were moved to set up their own federal machinery, the National Association of Building Trades Council, inaugurated in February 1915. Initially, as W. S. Hilton points out, it was little more " than a loose collection of executives with the primary aim of association on a narrow front against the threat of opposition."

In 1916 the N.A.B.T.C. (to which the Plumbers were affiliated) arranged for a special meeting to consider a scheme for federation that had been drawn up by the Amalgamated Society of Carpenters and Joiners. The scheme had one clear advantage over previous efforts in the same direction: it recognised the fact that most of the building craft unions were wholeheartedly in favour of closer unity but were not willing to sacrifice their individual rights and identities in order to achieve it. The Carpenters' scheme was eventually endorsed by the N.A.B.T.C., which met for the last time in February 1918 to pass the following resolution: " This building trades council be, and the same is hereby, dissolved from this date, and those societies who have voted in favour of the federation scheme are hereby formed as the National Federation of Building Trades Operatives."

The objects of the young Federation were " to uphold the rights of combination of labour; to consolidate the unions for mutual protection; the adjustment of disputes that may arise; to provide financial support in times of strikes or lockouts; to improve the general position and status of the workers by securing unity of action amongst the societies forming the federation." Affiliation fees were fixed at 6d. per member and contributions at 2d. per member per quarter. The Secretary was W. Bradshaw of the Stonemasons, and John Edmiston was Treasurer.

By the summer of 1918 Lachlan MacDonald had left

hospital and was fit enough to resume his duties at G.O. No sooner had he done so, however, than Edmiston—a much older man—broke down under the strain imposed upon him through the weary years of the war. He was given three months' leave of absence but the damage was too deep and he resigned at the end of the year. In the second ballot for the election of his successor, Lachlan MacDonald defeated J. L. Smyth of Birkenhead; Smyth subsequently followed MacDonald into the office as Assistant General Secretary.

A few months before hostilities ended, no less than one quarter of U.O.P.A. members were in uniform; over 300 died in battle. Printed reports in the months following the Armistice contained rows of photographs of members included on the Association's " Roll of Honour." War-time scarcities of essential commodities had forced up prices to unprecedented levels and wages soon began to follow. In February 1918 the hourly rate for plumbers ranged from 1s. to 1s. 4d. In March there was a notable increase at Dundee of 4d. an hour. By the end of the year wages were soaring throughout the country.

One of the outstanding milestones in the Union's history bears the date 1919. With the end of the war came the urgent need to call delegates together for the meeting deferred from 1917: a meeting which would be faced with the responsibility of deciding how far the U.O.P.A. should be remodelled on the lines laid down at the special conference. On this occasion the challenge was met and accepted with commendable courage. The hesitation, the half-hearted approaches of earlier Delegate Meetings to urgent demands for reforms of direction and administration, were seldom in evidence as the Plumbers, emerging from war-time darkness, set their house in order and faced a new peace with resolution.

The Banqueting Hall at Jesmond Dene, Newcastle, was the melting pot into which was thrown much scrap metal dismantled from the Association's now creaking machine and from which was cast the structure of a new trade union—a structure that was to endure until the next major overhaul at the end of World War II.

Lachlan MacDonald was again prominent as one of the draughtsmen of the new organisation, which was to be known as The Amalgamated Society of Plumbers, Domestic Engineers and Kindred Trades of Great Britain and Ireland— a title that was never adopted because of subsequent failure to secure the endorsement of two-thirds of the membership as required by law for registration purposes. But this was only a trivial failure. In the light of the revolutionary amendments to rule which were effected by the 1919 D.M. one can only regard with incredulity the formidable task confronting the Association's administrators, who were, after all, still amateurs in the sense that they had only the rudiments of the knowledge and experience required to translate ideas and proposals into the clarity demanded of rules which must not only be expressive of the D.M.'s intentions but acceptable for legal endorsement. Nevertheless, the task was accomplished. General Office was to be established in London as the Association's permanent headquarters and there was to be a full-time National Executive Council of seven members plus a General Managing President, G.S. and A.G.S., all of whom would be elected by ballot vote of the U.O.P.A. members. Candidates for any of these positions would be required to present manifestoes to the membership setting out their industrial and political views. District organisation, too, was put on a more professional basis. Rules were framed to permit the election of full-time District Secretaries, who would hold office for three years and draw a salary between £5 and £6 a week. South Shields delegates introduced a rule giving official recognition to shop stewards inside the Association; these were to be appointed by District Committees and issued with credentials.

Possibly the most important decision of all, however, was the abandoning of the antiquated system of " equalisation " of funds which had survived for over fifty years. The General Fund was established. Seventy-five per cent of all Lodge balances were to be forwarded to G.O. and banked in this Fund in the name of the Association. This change-over from local to central finance, in itself, required a drastic overhaul of the administrative and clerical methods. Nevertheless, without it much of the other good work done at Jesmond

THE EXECUTIVE COUNCIL IN SESSION, 1931

P. Walsh (nearest camera), *George H. Harris* (A.G.S.), *John W. Stephenson* (G.S.), *F. Hoey*
T. McKenna, T. McMenemy and J. W. Pickford

EXECUTIVE COUNCIL AND GENERAL OFFICERS, 1946

Hugh Kelly,   G. H. Morgan,   T. McMenemy,   H. W. Newman,
Geo. H. Harris (A.G.S.),   P. Walsh,   J. W. Stephenson (G.S.)

Dene would have been rendered ineffectual. Just how far
the outlook of the Plumbers had advanced since pre-war times
may be judged from the suggestion that full-time Lodge Secretaries should also be introduced for Lodges with over 200
members. This proposal, however, was too *avant-garde* for
even the U.O.P.A. to accept at the 1919 D.M.

Jesmond Dene's flood-tide of progress also swept into the
rule book several other features now familiar to our members.
The Standing Orders Committee was in future to be elected
from the membership by ballot vote (not from the delegates
attending the D.M.); so, too, were the Association's representatives to the Annual Congress of the T.U.C.

The interval between Delegate Meetings was once again
revised; this time it was reduced to three years. Delegates
reluctantly acknowledged that an impasse had been reached
in relations with the Heating Engineers and decided that " in
view of the impossibility of amalgamation, all D.C.s and
Lodges arrange meetings and working agreements." There
were also signs of growing dissatisfaction with the implications
of the U.O.P.A.'s affiliation to the N.F.B.T.O., since it was
widely felt that this stultified the traditional freedom of the
U.O.P.A. to negotiate separately in the various districts with
the Master Plumbers. Feeling was so strong on this issue,
in fact, that it was decided to ask the N.F.B.T.O. to declare
themselves in favour of local settlements by individual trades;
if no satisfactory assurance to this effect was given by the
Federation, the question of secession from the N.F.B.T.O.
would be put to a vote of the U.O.P.A. members.

The Plumbers' irritation was exacerbated by the fact that
the Ministry of Labour refused to recognise the N.J.I.C. for
the Plumbing Trade (formed in 1915) as a negotiating body,
although the Council had already made history by reaching
agreement early in 1919 for the introduction of a 44-hour
working week for plumbers from the beginning of April.
The N.F.B.T.O. had been working to the same end, but on a
regional basis. Once again a conflict developed between the
sincere desire of most U.O.P.A. members for effective federation in the building industry and the strong disinclination to
surrender the rights and privileges of craft individuality which
had been so jealously safeguarded over the years.

J

Relations with the N.F.B.T.O. deteriorated rapidly in the early months of 1920, and after some inconclusive discussions the Executive Council submitted to the U.O.P.A. members two alternatives in an attempt to secure a decisive, but clumsy solution to what in point of fact was a very complex and delicate problem. Was the U.O.P.A. to throw in its lot with the Federation and accept for its members the rates of wages and industrial conditions negotiated between the N.F.B.T.O. and the Master Builders, or was it to continue to champion plumbers as an individual craft through the medium of the N.J.C. for the Plumbing Trade? Members voted firmly in favour of the latter. Accordingly, the U.O.P.A. gave six months' notice to the Federation of their decision to withdraw.

Fortunately, the threatened break never occurred. Common sense emerged victorious and a compromise formula was worked out with the N.F.B.T.O. in which they agreed that " where Plumbers are now receiving wages above the flat (building) rate, their wages in such places shall not be interfered with as a result of them remaining in the Federation. But in subsequent applications for advances it must be distinctly understood that the Plumbers shall be brought into line with other Federated trades." The Federation later confirmed that this formula would not prevent a plumber accepting a rate in excess of the flat rate, providing it was not the result of an " organised effort " and that no Federation machinery was involved. Thus the delicate balance between the Plumbers' conflcting desires for unity on the one hand and individuality on the other was temporarily maintained

The most encouraging event in 1920 was the final reunification of Scottish and English plumbers. For nearly fifty years the U.O.P.A. of Scotland had ploughed its lonely furrow, until by the end of 1918 it had about 1,000 members and total funds of approximately £5,000. A vote of the Scottish members at the end of the war had already endorsed joint proposals for amalgamation, and delegates at Jesmond Dene in 1919 had little hesitation in recommending U.O.P.A. members to do likewise. The last enemy to amalgamation—

apathy—was not easily defeated, but at the second attempt
the Plumbers managed to secure the requisite number of votes
to make the fusion of the two estranged societies legally
acceptable. The merger became effective on 1st January,
1921.

Amalgamation was also the objective in talks being held
during this period between leaders of the U.O.P.A. and those
of the A.E.U. and the Coppersmiths Society. Relations with
the Heating Engineers, however, showed no signs of improvement. The Engineering and Shipbuilding Trades' Federation
had incurred the extreme displeasure of the Plumbers by
making a national arbitration award declaring that all lead
work for hot and cold water supplies and services was
plumbers' work, but work in hard metals such as iron, brass
and copper could be claimed equally by plumbers or heating
engineers. The Arbitration Court had been set up by the
E. and S. Federation as a result of sporadic disputes between
the two trades in certain regions, and in spite of vehement
protests by the U.O.P.A. that such disputes should be settled
by *local* arbitration. J. L. Smyth (A.G.S.) and S. Sigsworth
(G.M.P.) attended the Court but refused to submit evidence,
confining themselves to the contention that the Court's
appointment was a direct contravention of the rules of the
Federation. On this point the U.O.P.A. stood firm; on this
foundation they based their absolute refusal to acknowledge
the validity of the ultimate award of the Arbitration Court,
which had " ridden roughshod over the Rules of the E. and
S.B. Federation," as Lachlan MacDonald declared.

Once again, as in the past, the Plumbers turned to the
employers for moral support in resisting the gradual erosion
of their work. At the end of 1920 they issued a letter to
plumbing employers underlining the urgent need for " those
engaged in the Plumbing Industry to stand together in order
to preserve the work for the industry." Each firm was asked
to complete a questionnaire with descriptions of work undertaken within the compass of hot and cold domestic supplies,
with the names of plumbers who had carried it out. In
notifying this action to the members, the E.C. also revealed
that the Ministry of Labour had intervened in an attempt to
find a solution to the differences between the two associations.

" All efforts to arrive at a reasonable settlement with the Heating Engineers have failed," said Lachlan MacDonald, " and they seem to be prepared to take all they can get and keep asking for more."

Correspondence then began with the T.U.C. General Council, and arrangements were made for a conference to promote the amalgamation of plumbers and heating engineers. No progress could be made because each side stuck doggedly to its own line of approach: the U.O.P.A. refused point blank to discuss a national demarcation agreement, while the Heating Engineers declined to attend any meetings on amalgamation. Finally, in October 1922 the Plumbers' reluctantly agreed to send representatives to a conference convened jointly by the Master Builders, Master Plumbers, Master Heating Engineers and the N.F.B.T.O. They had no alternative but to yield to the pressure of the convening authorities, who declared that the conference would take place with or without the U.O.P.A., and its recommendations, whatever they might be, would be observed. Clearly this challenge could not be ignored, although the Plumbers still maintained that they had T.U.C. backing for talks on amalgamation and not on demarcation.

The result of the October conference was the setting up of a small committee under the chairmanship of an architect, Mr. Paul Waterhouse, for the purpose of discussing " with all parties concerned the avenues of conciliation by amalgamation, arbitration or conciliation, and that an amicable settlement be arrived at." After a good deal of skirmishing the following agreement was reached: " That the Heating Engineers will submit to their Executive the advisability of taking a ballot of their members as to whether they shall be allowed to discuss amalgamation with the Plumbers' Association, provided that the Plumbers' Association are prepared to take a ballot of their members on the straight issue as to whether they can discuss demarcation on a national basis. One ballot to be conditional on the other being taken." This feeble, face-saving formula could hardly have been regarded by either side as an indication that a settlement of the crucial problem was imminent.

CHAPTER VIII

THE DESPERATE YEARS OF PEACE

MEANWHILE, national events were becoming worse and worse. Gone was the rosy prospect of peace and plenty and a land " fit for heroes " which had probably fired the imaginations of thousands of workers returning from the Flanders mud after the guns fell silent. Disillusionment swept the industrial scene: economic disaster again hovered on the British horizon. As W. S. Hilton comments in *Foes to Tyranny*: " The impetus of war was gone. Unemployment began to rise as quickly as the cost-of-living index went down. The bitter rearguard struggles of the building unions, against the attacks of the employers, were now being echoed throughout the entire country as miners and other workers fought to prevent poverty and degradation being inflicted upon them as their ' reward ' for winning the war. But they were almost as powerless to resist the onslaught of the employers who were now taking retribution for the concessions wrung from them in better times."

A national lock-out in the shipbuilding industry in March 1922, was followed almost immediately by another in the engineering industry. The shipbuilding employers proposed wage reductions amounting to 26s. 6d. a week; after acrimonious exchanges the E. and S. Federation finally accepted reductions of 16s. 6d. a week after a vote of members of affiliated unions, while rejecting the offer of the Employers, had not provided the two-thirds majority required by a Federation rule to allow the strike to continue. Shipyard workers returned dejectedly to their yards in May. All along the line the Plumbers' Executive had urged total rejection of the employers' demands, but when all trades finally resumed work " there is no alternative but to instruct our members to do the same."

The forthright opposition of the U.O.P.A. was equally fruitless in the engineering dispute. By almost exactly two to one, members affiliated to the E. and S. Federation voted against the acceptance of proposed reductions in " war bonuses " which would effectively reduce engineering wages by the same amount as in the shipbuilding industry. Even when a Court of Inquiry was set up and employers reopened their gates for a resumption of work, the E.C. warned members " against this insidious move on the part of the employers." As might be expected in the circumstances of the times, however, the workers were ultimately forced to fall in line, if only to save themselves from utter destitution. Work began again in June 1922.

In the building industry the picture was very similar, although a national conflict with the employers had been avoided. By this time a large measure of uniformity of wages had been achieved throughout the country by means of the National Wages and Conditions Council, forerunner of the N.J.C. for the Building Industry. Through the machinery of this Council, to which the N.F.B.T.O. and Master Builders were parties, wages moved in step with the cost of living index on lines now familiar to all building trade workers. Within the space of two years the Grade " A " hourly rate fell from 2s. 4d. to 1s. 8d.—a drop of nearly 30 per cent. Not until 1946 was it to reach the level it touched in 1920.

From what has gone before it will be obvious that the Plumbers had always had their doubts as to the value of federation. Experiences in Victorian days in Cardiff and elsewhere, when they had stood solidly side by side with other building crafts through bitter disputes only to find ultimate disillusionment, had inculcated in the trade union plumber an understandable caution in his attitude to federal action. Nevertheless, in the 1920s the U.O.P.A. found itself affiliated to the N.F.B.T.O. and, indirectly, to the Engineering and Shipbuilding Trades' Federation. But the desire to " go it alone " was never far below the surface. We have seen how close they came in 1920 to rejecting the N.F.B.T.O.: in the summer of 1921 they drew no comfort from the Master Plumbers' decision to accept a seat on the National Wages and Conditions Council, thereby accepting the principle of the national regulation of building trade wages by that body. Towards the end of the following year, after U.O.P.A. members had narrowly rejected any association with the N.W.C.C., came a joint declaration by the Master Plumbers and Master Builders to the effect that local rates for plumbers would be abolished from 1st May, 1923, after which N.W.C.C. rates would be universally applied. This decision had already been foreshadowed in 1922 by a constitutional amendment from the Building Trade Employers seeking to bring plumbers' wages into line with those of the N.W.C.C.

The E.C. rightly felt that "every man's hand was turned against them." Final defeat had to be acknowledged when a Manchester member's County Court claim for the difference between local Reference Board (Plumbing J.I.C.) rates and N.W.C.C. rates paid to him by his employer failed completely. The U.O.P.A. was federated; and after the "Lord Mayor's Show" at the time of affiliation now followed the unpleasant but inevitable reality.

Faced with soaring unemployment, widespread industrial unrest, tumbling wages, deepening hostility towards the heating engineers, and a host of minor afflictions, the U.O.P.A. had trouble enough when preparations began in the Spring of 1922 for another Delegate Meeting. Even so, the harsh truth was like an iceberg: seven-eighths of it was concealed beneath the surface.

As a result of the heavy financial demands made on Association funds partly by the disruptions of the early 'twenties and partly by some sincere but thoughtless decisions at Jesmond Dene (concealed, perhaps, by the progressive renovations to the Association's structure), the Plumbers came closer to bankruptcy in the ensuing years than at any time in their history. The flood of expenditure can best be appreciated by a survey of strike benefit figures for the immediate post-war years. In 1919—£9,960; in 1920—£14,712; in 1921—£41,276, leaving the U.O.P.A. with a net overall deficit of £34,500 for that year. In 1922—£52,148. Unemployment benefit also rocketed from £3,600 in 1920 to £31,000 the following year and to £41,300 for 1922. The 1922 disputes in engineering and shipbuilding alone cost the Association about £45,000; for the first six months of that year nearly £83,000 went out in benefits while only £52,000 came in. The United Operative Plumbers Association might well be a non-profit-making organisation, but there was obviously no future in this degree of philanthropy.

Indications of serious financial difficulties were already apparent early in 1922 when a suggestion that representation to the forthcoming D.M. should be on a District basis instead of a Lodge basis was readily accepted. Lachlan MacDonald pointed out that by reducing the number of delegates from 280 to 90 this proposal would thereby reduce expenditure on fares and expenses from about £4,000 to £1,400. At the same time came an announcement that strike benefit, raised from 15s. to £2 a week by the 1919 D.M., was to be halved until further notice. The reasons for this drastic decision are not hard to find: from a total of £38,000 at the end of March 1922 the Reserve Fund balance had diminished to the paltry figure of £3,100 by early May.

By September the position was worse. Further severe measures were put forward to the members, and MacDonald declared: " Brothers, the E.C. appeals to you all to stand fast to the Association. The whole trade movement is being attacked by the most powerful federation of Employers ever brought into existence. Our Association is standing today at the parting of the ways. On all sides we are attacked by skilled and semi-skilled members of other unions . . . and all and sundry who can screw a piece of pipe or attempt to carry out our work. Our Association is not of mushroom growth; its achievements are as creditable as those of any other union. If we go down, in ten years our trade will be in the hands of others and the birthright handed down to us will have been frittered away. Our duty . . . is to appreciate as men that it is no use cringing before adversity. Stand fast, hold on, keep the organisation intact and we can look to the future with confidence."

The Executive's proposals were two-fold: a reduction in administrative expenses and a reduction in benefits. There was to be a ten per cent cut in all salaries of E.C., General Officers and District Secretaries, and in Lodge management allowances. Sickness Benefit was to be cut by 1s. a week and Out-of-work Benefit by 1s. 6d. a week. Strike Benefit would continue at half the prescribed rate.

When the members' response was known there must have

been cynical smiles in the Board Room—and some unprintable comments. The cuts in salaries were endorsed, but the proposed reductions in benefits were rejected.

By this time, of course, the full-time National Executive Council was in monthly session at the Association's new permanent headquarters in Abbeville Road, Clapham, having met for the first time in Newcastle on 16th October, 1920. Its members were W. J. Pickford of Bristol, Fred Hoey of Liverpool No. 1, T. McKenna of Newcastle, E. J. Shea of Cardiff, T. McMenemy of Glasgow Govan, C. R. Worling of Aberdeen and James Walker of Belfast. Septimus Sigsworth of South Shields was "Grand Managing President." This team, unchanged except for the death of James Walker at the June E.C. meeting in 1923, carried the U.O.P.A. through the triumphant rally at Jesmond Dene. Moreover, it faced plans of 1919 were brutally shattered and the Association was brought almost to death's door.

When the fourteenth Delegate Meeting opened in the Church Hall, Hambalt Road, Clapham, on 10th April, 1923, it must have seemed a modest affair by comparison with the triumphant rally at Jesmond Dene. Moreover, it faced an extremely unenviable task. In view of the Association's mounting poverty, delegates had to determine not only the future policy of the U.O.P.A. on such complex problems as its relations with the N.F.B.T.O. and the Heating Engineers, but also the extent to which the revolutionary changes made in 1919 could be extended, maintained—or even rescinded. There was general agreement that benefits, so liberally increased four years before, must be pruned severely to meet the financial circumstances. Strike Benefit was confirmed at the figure of £1 a week, while unemployment benefit was slashed to 10s. a week for 10 weeks only and superannuation benefit (doubled at Jesmond Dene) was reduced to realistic limits with a maximum of 9s. a week for members with 40 years' membership who joined after 1912. The Table A contribution came down from 1s. 9d. to 1s. 5d.—a natural corollary to the fall in wages since 1919.

Delegates finally swept aside the "craft" inhibitions of their predecessors by deciding that the Association "should be extended to embrace all those who earn their livelihood at

the plumbing trade or any branch of it." As an earnest of
their intentions they agreed to change the title of the union
to " The Amalgamated Society of Plumbers, Domestic
Engineers and Allied Trades of Great Britain and Ireland."
Once again the decision was later to be thwarted by the
failure to fulfil the legal requirements of the Trade Union
Act in regard to voting figures.

For the first time, E.C. salaries were linked on a percentage
basis to the " prevailing rate paid to members in the London
District." The Industrial Table was established, and among
the members of the new-style Standing Orders Committee
(elected by a ballot vote of all members) was J. W. Stephenson
of Newcastle.

While the D.M. was in progress at Clapham, a crisis
developed in the building industry. The threat of a nation-
wide strike against the Employers' proposed wage reductions
and extension of working hours was averted only a few
hours before lock-out notices were due to take effect, when
the two sides agreed (following an intervention by Ramsay
MacDonald himself) that the issues should be sent to arbitration. The gravity of events cannot have failed to influence
the Delegate Meeting in its approach to the Association's
domestic problems, not least of which was the widespread
reluctance of members to accept once and for all the full
implications of federation. To " go it alone " was no longer
feasible: but the heads of many remained beneath the sand.

Less than three months after the D.M. had dispersed,
further unpleasant measures had to be taken to maintain the
Association's solvency. There was a deficit of nearly £6,000
on the General Fund: a bank overdraft was secured and
£4,000 was borrowed from the Reserve Fund to cover the cost
of the D.M. Matters were not ameliorated by a protracted
lock-out of boilermakers which involved U.O.P.A. members
and sustained a steady out-flow of benefit. By November
1923 the need for economy was so desperate that the issue of
published reports was suspended indefinitely. Even worse
was to follow before the U.O.P.A. was assured of survival.

Meanwhile, relations with the Heating Engineers were as bad as ever. Both Associations had taken the votes recommended by the Waterhouse Committee and both memberships had endorsed the opponent's proposals. A joint meeting of Executive Councils followed, when it was agreed that the Plumbers would draw up amalgamation proposals while the Heating Engineers would draft a scheme for national demarcation. Then another impasse was reached. The Heating Engineers declined to supply certain details of membership and finance requested by the U.O.P.A. for the purpose of working out the plans for amalgamation. "The Executive desire to make it quite plain," wrote Lachlan MacDonald in January 1924, " that there has been no truce with the Heating Engineers. The questions of amalgamation and demarcation are being held up by the refusal of the Heating Engineers to supply essential information."

In the same month the death occurred of one of the Association's most respected members who had served the U.O.P.A. loyally and conscientiously as its leading advocate: John H. Edmiston. Future difficulties in the gas industry were foreshadowed by an eight-month strike of Nottingham members in their dispute with the local Gas Committee over negotiating rights. The E.C. maintained that the U.O.P.A. was entitled to a seat on the N.J.C. for the Gas Industry, which determined the rates and conditions of the gas workers. In spite of support from the N.F.B.T.O., however, little headway was made; and although the employers kept their promise (on which a resumption of work was secured) to call a special conference to examine the problem, there is no indication that any positive steps were taken to meet the Plumbers' claim.

At the same time, another upheaval occurred in the building industry. In response to a claim by the operatives for an increase of 2d. an hour the employers had offered a halfpenny and there were clear indications that the two sides were heading for trouble. On 16th June, 1924, however, union representatives accepted the employers' offer on the understanding that (among other things) a Joint Committee would be set up to enquire into the problem of time lost through bad weather (" wet time ") and the adjustment of working hours in relation to the state of employment. The matter appeared to have been settled. Four days later came the employers' bombshell: they withdrew their offer, broke off negotiations and declared a lock-out from 5th July. The N.F.B.T.O. decided that the lock-out must take its course and every effort should be made in the regions to secure settlements based on the original offer, subject to endorsement by the joint Executives.

The lock-out was a body blow to the U.O.P.A., still financially groggy from the effects of the long and costly disputes of 1922 in engineering and shipbuilding and expenditure of £107,000 in strike benefit during 1923. They were obviously in no position to face further debilitating expense, although as Lachlan MacDonald pointed out, " we are still committed to the N.F.B.T.O. and must, therefore, carry out the policy and general instructions issued by that body as regards the dispute." As the lock-out commenced, the E.C. made some hurried calculations and a snap decision: " It is anticipated that 10,000 of our members will be involved at the outset, but of that number 2,000 will be enabled to remain at work as a result of local or regional agreements, together with those in employment of Public Authorities, etc. . . . thus leaving 8,000 members to be provided with Strike Benefit. It is impossible to pay the full amount of Strike Benefit stipulated in General Rule, consequently it was agreed that payment . . . be at the rate of 10s. per week on and from Monday, 7th July, 1924." A levy of 1s. per week was imposed on all members, with those remaining at work at the higher rate paying an additional levy equivalent to the weekly increase in wages.

It was all very well for the E.C. to impose emergency levies—which, in the event, were never collected: the immediate problem was the drain on funds in payment of lock-out benefit, which even at the reduced rate would exhaust the Reserve Fund in less than a month. In such a situation, how could the Association avoid utter disaster?

There was only one answer, and it is to the credit of the U.O.P.A. leaders that they recognised it, left their pride at home and took immediate action. The assistance of other, more wealthy unions was sought and was granted to the extent of over £15,000 free of interest. Those who threw a financial lifeline to the U.O.P.A. included the N.U.R., the Railway Clerks' Association, the Woodworkers, the Sailors' and Firemen's Union and the N.F.B.T.O., so demonstrating in the most practical manner that the true spirit of trade unionism was far from being extinguished.

After seven weeks a formula was found for reopening negotiations and building workers resumed work on 25th August. It was to be nearly 40 years before the industry faced another national disruption. The scars left on the U.O.P.A. by the 1924 dispute were not only financial; Liverpool building members, who had always maintained their own separate arrangements with the employers until May 1924, had taken strong exception to the employers' decision that there should be complete uniformity throughout the country and that Liverpool operatives should thus be brought within the ambit of the N.W.C.C. This would have meant an immediate reduction in wages and changes in working conditions. Merseyside operatives, including the plumbers, would have none of this nonsense and withdrew their labour on 28th June—a week before the national lock-out.

The E.C. stubbornly refused to pay Strike Benefit—not only for the week of the " unofficial " withdrawal on Merseyside but for the subsequent seven weeks of lock-out as well. Liverpool No. 1 Lodge members countered by refusing to pay the Reserve Fund levy. Matters went from bad to worse until in October the E.C. took charge of the Lodge and warned the members that unless they paid the levy in accordance with rule they would be excluded. In December, officers of Birkenhead Lodge declined to collect any further Union contributions and their colleagues " over the water " followed suit. Some degree of reconciliation was eventually achieved; in March 1925 the E.C. placed before the membership the Lodge's appeal for payment of the disputed benefit. The vote went overwhelmingly in favour of the Liverpool members.

But the damage was done. Many disgruntled Merseyside members could not be placated and chose to sever their connections with the U.O.P.A. to join the rival organisation which had emerged from the dispute, known officially as " The National Operative Plumbers and Kindred Trades Union " and unofficially as the " Liverpool Locals." As in the case of the Scottish breakaway, the breach took many years to heal; not until December 1953 were all the Merseyside rebels reunited with the national organisation.

The building industry lock-out of 1924 also brought to a head the rising discontent of the building unions with the existing industrial machinery, and in particular with the National Wages and Conditions Council. Pressure from the rank and file persuaded certain unions, including the Plumbers, to make a reappraisal of the value of their affiliation to the N.F.B.T.O. In the A.U.B.T.W., for example, feeling ran so high that members voted by nearly eight to one in favour of secession, with the result that in the words of W. S. Hilton in *Foes to Tyranny*, " the union which had constantly preached closer unity between all of the organisations in the building industry now entered on a self-imposed four years' exile from its comrades within the Federation." The Plumbers, as always, were more cautious; perhaps they paid heed to the words of Lachlan MacDonald, who told them that " the Executive Council are of the opinion that the troubles which would arise if we withdrew from the N.F.B.T.O. would be disastrous to the interests of the members of our Association." Perhaps they also remembered that the Federation had given them a helping hand in their financial distress. At any rate, they voted to remain " in unity."

The building unions did, however, act in unison by withdrawing from the N.W.C.C. early in 1925 in accordance with an Annual Conference decision of the Federation. A sub-committee of the Council was charged with the task of drawing up a new constitution and machinery for the regulation of building trade wages and conditions. By July, the committee had completed its work and affiliated unions were asked to endorse the draft constitution, rules and regulations of the new body, to be known as The National Joint Council for the Building Industry.

The Plumbers' E.C. had little stomach for it. " Your Executive strenuously opposed the document for the reason that national wage negotiations is still a feature of it," declared the G.S. Having made the point that the U.O.P.A. were still the champions of local negotiations, however, MacDonald continued: " They now feel they have no alternative but to recommend our members to vote in favour of acceptance. In arriving at this decision they have been influenced largely by their experience in the past, when our Association stood out against joining the N.W.C.C. until such time as they were forced by the decision of Judge Hogge at Manchester to recognise the authority of the N.W.C.C. They have no desire that history should repeat itself in so far that your wages and conditions of labour should be governed by a body with which you have no act or part. Finding all the unions ranged against them, they feel constrained to recommend the document now before you because in their opinion it is the best arrangement you can have when all the circumstances are considered."

In spite of the Plumbers' lukewarm reception, the National Joint Council was generally regarded as a far more effective instrument of joint negotiation than its predecessor.

While the building unions were reshaping their negotiating machinery the U.O.P.A. was simultaneously engaged in talks with the Plumbing Employers. Relations between the two sides had been somewhat distant since the Master Plumbers had thrown in their lot with the Building Trade employers and joined the N.W.C.C. some years earlier. Accepting the fact that " there were many other matters upon which the Employers and the U.O.P.A. could meet and consider with profit to the trade as a whole," the E.C. set before the members for approval the proposed new constitution for the N.J.I.C. for the Plumbing Trade. One of the objects was to secure " the greatest possible measure of joint action between Employers and Employees for the development of the trade, to raise its status and to improve the conditions of all engaged therein." Any consideration of wages and conditions of work was specifically excluded. The new constitution was ratified in December 1925.

In the same year Lachlan MacDonald was re-elected General Secretary on the first ballot against four challengers who included the A.G.S., J. L. Smyth, and George H. Harris of Manchester No. 2. Shortly after his re-election he issued a hard-hitting attack on the " Liverpool Locals " in rebuttal to a leaflet distributed by that society after a dispute at Walton. The leaflet had been signed by a " rebel " who later became one of the Union's most respected officials—Alex Johnson.

Britain's most violent and controversial industrial catastrophe was imminent. There was a hint of the coming tragedy in the final words of Stanley Baldwin to a meeting with the Miners on 30th July, 1925: " All the workers of this country have got to face a reduction of wages." The mentality of the mineowners and their supporters in Parliament appears to have sunk to the same level as that of the early nineteenth century industrialists who fought so tenaciously to prevent the repeal of the Combination Acts. The explosion occurred in May 1926. No repetition is needed here of the grim events of the nine-day General Strike which brought the British people closer to civil war than at any time since the days of Cromwell and subsequently brought the Labour Party to the brink of internal destruction. The U.O.P.A., in spite of its precarious domestic situation, showed no hesitation in placing its resources entirely at the disposal of the T.U.C. General Council. Once more the Plumbers had secured less than two years' breathing space between one financial crisis and the next. Nevertheless, it was " business as usual."

As remarkable as the Association's continued survival, perhaps, is the fact that only four months after the General Strike another Delegate Meeting was held. True, the E.C. had proposed its cancellation, but the members would not hear of it. Representation had been restricted even further by a vote taken in September 1925 and expenses were kept down by again holding the D.M. at the Parochial Hall, Oldridge Road, Balham—a stone's throw from General Office. It was only to be expected that the 1926 D.M. would concentrate on measures designed to assist the Association in regaining some semblance of financial stability. " We cannot continue as we are doing now," said Lachlan MacDonald in his report. " We must either find more money to meet our liabilities or we must curtail our expenditure. Which is it to be?"

Which, indeed? He had already revealed that the balance in the General Fund, standing at £18,250 in June 1923, had dropped to £4,200 by the end of 1925, in spite of the imposition of an emergency levy of 6d. a week on all members and the continuation of the 1s. per week Reserve Fund levy. Membership was also on the wane; at the end of 1925 it stood at 23,864, a fall of nearly 500 since 1923. " It will be within your recollection," the G.S. told the delegates, " that payments made of £2 and £1 per week respectively for lock-out benefit, whilst in accordance with General Rule, frittered away our funds to such an extent that when we required the money for disputes with which we were directly concerned there was not sufficient to foot the bill."

Notwithstanding these exhortations, the D.M. confined its economy measures mainly to the Association's structure and administration. The number of full-time Executive Officers was cut to five and the office of G.M.P. was abolished. The Executive would in future meet quarterly and only two of their number would attend the Delegate Meeting, which was to assemble at five-yearly instead of three-yearly intervals on the basis of the reduced representation already accepted for 1926. The Standing Orders Committee was also reduced to a five-man team. A Committee of Enquiry was set up to investigate G.O. administrative procedures and the work of the Executive Council, apparently with the dual purpose of pruning headquarters' expenses as far as possible and making recommendations for increased efficiency.

The only significant alteration to the Association's benefits was the establishment of a special fund for payment of Superannuation Benefit to be maintained by a transfer of 6s. per member per annum from contributions and an extra levy of 2d. a week on all members eligible for this benefit.

When members voted early in 1927 for their new officers, four of the retiring Executive Council were re-elected on the first vote; J. W. Pickford, Fred Hoey, T. McKenna and P. Walsh of Dublin, who had succeeded the late James Walker as E.C. Officer for Ireland. Scottish members, however, who

K

had had two representatives on the old E.C., needed three ballots before finally sending back Tommy McMenemy in preference to C. R. Worling of Aberdeen.

The year of the General Strike saw the re-election of J. L. Smyth as A.G.S. and the adoption of a well-known Belfast member, G. M. Donaldson, as a Parliamentary candidate. For the first time, too, the U.O.P.A. published the " *Plumbers' Own Diary* "; the charge to members was 8d. each.

The Heating Engineers, of course, were still in the news. To delegates at the 1926 D.M., Lachlan MacDonald submitted a 13-page " short " history of relations between the two organisations and current developments in the apparently endless search for peace. MacDonald made no attempt to disguise his belief that justice was on the side of the Plumbers, however delicate the situation might be at that point in time. " The plumber from time immemorial has been the craftsman who has handled water supplies and as time progressed we find systems developed for conveying hot water about buildings by means of water pipes. To cover the whole evolution of the progress of heating water for domestic supply would require a special treatise; it will be sufficient for our purpose to say that from the very first systems used, the plumber has been employed to fix and maintain them. The Plumbers' Union have records going back to 1832 that show that plumbers had the exclusive monopoly of all work in hot or cold water until the introduction of hard metal piping. The men who were in conflict with the plumber were not regarded as being eligible for membership of the Plumbers' Union, and in fact were mostly whitesmiths, locksmiths and general iron-workers." He also revealed that the heating engineers' national society had been established in 1908, only a year before the notorious " Leicester Award " given by a Board of Trade arbitrator, Alderman T. Smith; this award had declared that in the water area of the Leicester Corporation all lead-pipe work for hot and cold water supplies and services and all domestic waste, soil and ventilating pipes were plumbers' work, but that other work for heating, ventilation and hot and cold supplies in iron, brass, copper or other hard metals could be done either by plumbers or heating engineers as might be provided by contractors' specifications. Time and again this award had been used against the U.O.P.A. all over the country.

It will be remembered that in 1924 the U.O.P.A. were met with a blank refusal by the other union when they requested certain information for the purpose of drawing up amalgamation plans at the same time as the Heating Engineers were drafting a scheme for national demarcation. In February 1925 the Waterhouse Committee of 1922 was recalled. Plumbers' representatives complained bitterly that while the votes of the two associations were being taken on the twin propositions of amalgamation and demarcation, the Heating Engineers at their triennial conference had altered their rules in such a way that the amalgamation of the two bodies was virtually impossible. Their revised rule stated: " Any Society of trades mentioned in the last paragraph, if approved by a majority of the members of this Society, may amalgamate with this Society. In which case the other Society shall hand over its books, box, cash and all other effects to the E.C. of this Society, which shall enter such Society on the books of this Society, whereupon they shall conform to these rules." At that time the Heating Engineers' membership was about 4,000, compared with 25,000 members in the U.O.P.A. Amalgamation? " Not — — — — likely," as Eliza Doolittle said.

In spite of their protests to the Waterhouse Committee the Plumbers had a bad day. They could not prevent the endorsement of a resolution which again put demarcation, conciliation or arbitration first and amalgamation a poor second and instructed the Executives of the two unions to set up a joint sub-committee to prepare a report on demarcation arrangements. In disgust, the Plumbers washed their hands of the whole proceedings. With the breakdown of existing negotiations the T.U.C. intervened once more and set up a Court of Inquiry, primarily to forestall the Ministry of Labour's declared intention to do likewise.

Delegates at the D.M. must surely have listened to the

General Secretary's report in that same sad silence that settles over conferences even today when bad news is being retailed from the platform. Their decision, however, was brief and unambiguous: the Plumbers were not to agree to any settlement unless it concerned amalgamation.

In the Spring of 1927 both parties met again at the T.U.C. and agreed to attend the Court of Inquiry, which had the following terms of reference: " To consider (a) amalgamation and (b) demarcation and to recommend any solution that might lead to a better understanding between the two Unions." After two meetings of the Court an agreement was reached providing for the establishment of the Joint Committee of both Executives for the purpose of drafting a demarcation agreement and appeals machinery, the holding of a special conference of the Heating Engineers to alter their amalgamation rule (conditional upon the demarcation agreement being accepted and put into operation), and for an undertaking by both sides that the Executives would recommend to their respective members and would work wholeheartedly for the amalgamation of the two societies.

This agreement was made on 16th November, 1927. By 19th January, 1928, after two joint meetings of both Executive Councils, deadlock had been reached once again. The Plumbers were firmly in favour of local demarcation arrangements: the Heating Engineers were equally adamant that national demarcation was the only solution. With due deference the baby was handed back to the T.U.C.

Although from the earliest days of the U.O.P.A. piecework had been a dirty word, the Association was partly committed by the 1922 Agreement between the Engineering Employers and the Engineering and Shipbuilding Federation to accept the P.B.R. principle in engineering, but it retained the right to challenge any attempt by individual employers to force U.O.P.A. members to participate in such schemes. At a conference with U.O.P.A. leaders in 1927, the Engineering Employers made it abundantly clear that if the Association continued its policy of refusing to allow members to take part in piecework schemes there was a grave danger that such plumbers would lose the work in question to other trades who were under no similar restrictions. The Plumbers' E.C. took the logical step of asking members to give them authority to " contract out " of the relevant General Rule so far as the engineering and shipbuilding industries were concerned, in order that plumbers would not be displaced by other men. In the light of the economic circumstances prevailing in 1927 it is hardly surprising that U.O.P.A. members endorsed the Executive's suggestion by a large majority.

Early in 1928 there was a change in the Plumbers' " general staff." J. L. Smyth resigned as A.G.S. in order to take up an appointment as head of the newly-created Social Insurance Department of the T.U.C. Executive Officers were again instructed to take turns in filling the gap for a month at a time until a new A.G.S. was elected. Among the original candidates were E. H. Dimond, later full-time District Secretary for South Wales, Executive Officers W. J. Pickford and Fred Hoey, George Harris of Manchester and John W. Stephenson, Newcastle District Secretary. Harris, Hoey and Stephenson went to the second ballot. The final contest was between Hoey and Stephenson, when the latter was the victor by 762 votes in a poll of over 10,000. He started work in G.O. in September 1928.

John Stephenson had scarely had time to take stock of his new surroundings than the General Secretary was taken seriously ill and granted two months' leave of absence. After a brief return to G.O. at the end of the year, Lachlan Mac-Donald died on 21st January, 1929, having led the United Operative Plumbers through one of their most desperate decades.

Three candidates stepped forward initially for the most important office in the Union, but such was the general confidence in the Association's young A.G.S. that George Harris and Fred Hoey withdrew from the contest, leaving John Walker Stephenson to be declared elected unopposed as General Secretary—a unique event in the annals of the U.O.P.A.

Another E.C. member, T. McKenna from the North-East Coast, joined his colleagues Pickford and Hoey in the ballot for A.G.S. in the early months of 1929; George H. Harris and G. M. Donaldson of Belfast were the other nominees. Hoey led Harris by about 450 votes on the first ballot, but in the final count George Harris emerged as the new A.G.S. with a majority of over 1,500.

Both newcomers to General Office were already well-known throughout the Association. John Stephenson had taken over the District Secretaryship in Newcastle only five years after his entry into the U.O.P.A. in 1915 and had served on the S.O.C. at the 1923 and 1926 Delegate Meetings; he was also a member of the special committee which attempted, unsuccessfuly, to secure a reconciliation with the " Liverpool Locals " in 1927. George H. Harris had already been a member of the U.O.P.A. for over 30 years when he came to G.O. in October 1929; after a year as secretary of Manchester No. 2 Lodge in 1908 he succeeded John H. Edmiston as full-time secretary for the combined Manchester Lodges and continued in that capacity (with a break for war service) until 1929. The administrative partnership of Stephenson and Harris was to continue for nearly twenty years.

CHAPTER IX

THE STRUGGLE FOR SURVIVAL

THE final year of Lachlan MacDonald's stewardship was marked by a complicated legal case involving two U.O.P.A. officials. Charges were brought against the secretary of Chester Lodge, John Kelly, and W. T. "Bill" Jones, Liverpool District Secretary, by the "Liverpool Locals." Subsequent Court proceedings became known as the "Chester Prosecution." Both members were charged under the Conspiracy and Protection of Property Act, 1875 and the Trade Disputes and Trade Union Act, 1927, with "watching and besetting certain premises with a view to compelling John Henry Langley to join the Plumbers' Union." Langley was a member of the breakaway society in Liverpool.

After some tortuous legal arguments at the Chester Quarter Sessions, Kelly was found not guilty and discharged. Bill Jones was less fortunate. At a later hearing he was convicted of intimidation and "watching and besetting" and fined £10. The Recorder, who bluntly admitted that he did not know the law himself, declared that if a non-unionist was visited by a trade union official, delegate or representative, either on the job or elsewhere, the very fact of the non-unionist knowing that the person visiting him was a trade union official was sufficient to enable him to claim that he had "a fear of damage or injury to himself in respect of his employment." A century after the legalisation of trade unions by the State, here was yet another example of the way in which current law—however ancient in origin—could be seized upon and interpreted to the detriment of the natural endeavours of trade union officers to fulfil one of their main functions: to make more members.

Two other events in 1928 are worth a mention. The 1926 D.M. had decided ("in their wisdom or otherwise" as the apologists might say) that candidates for full-time office in the U.O.P.A. should no longer be required to submit individual manifestoes. Instead, the Lodges nominating the particular candidate should state their reasons for so doing. The new system was first applied in the election of the five-man

Executive Council in 1927 and repeated in the ballot for A.G.S. after Smyth's resignation. The result was preposterous. Voting papers and the accompanying Lodge " adverts. " for their chosen candidate might well have been mistaken for a daily newspaper. After less than two years' experience of the practice, the E.C. decided it was a waste of money and sought the support of 20 Lodges for a vote on the proposal to revert to the old rule. The result was never in doubt. The necessary amendment to rule was approved by the Registrar in 1929.

Members were equally decisive when they voted on the Delegate Meeting's recommendation that the U.O.P.A. should establish a political fund. No doubt the political mess of the post-General Strike years, which left serious stains on the reputation of the Labour Party and its leaders, had some influence on the members' overwhelming decision to stay outside politics for the time being.

The entry of the United Operative Plumbers' Association into another decade was marked by events which, in the light of historic experience, must have appeared almost miraculous not only by their very nature but by the rapidity with which they occurred. For more than half a century, plumbers had been at odds with heating engineers and in spite of innumerable discussions, conferences, decisions, and appeals to the membership the problem had remained unresolved. After renewed deadlock in 1928, the T.U.C. had resumed their examination of the issues involved. Late in that year they recommended that the U.O.P.A. should secure the members' authority to accept certain fundamental principles: firstly, that a joint agreement should be signed by the two parties on the " main-line principles " of demarcation from which local agreements could be drawn up; secondly, that local agreements should be negotiated and put into effect; finally, that such local agreements should be merged into a national demarcation agreement. This was clearly an ingenious attempt to bridge the gap between the divergent views of the two organisations on the critical problem of demarcation.

Nevertheless, the Plumbers' E.C. objected to the formulation of "main-line principles"; their opinion was endorsed by the members, who rejected the T.U.C. proposals by nearly six to one. Was this the end of the road?

Pessimism was not alleviated by renewed disputes in 1929 between the two unions at Birmingham and elsewhere. The Heating Engineers applied to the T.U.C. for arbitration, thus presenting the U.O.P.A. with the dilemma of either accepting T.U.C. arbitration and subsequent findings, or ignoring the T.U.C. and leaving the other union to ask the Ministry of Labour to institute an inquiry under the Industrial Courts Act. But the Plumbers found a loophole: "believing that the Heating Engineering Employers are now more favourably inclined towards the view that amalgamation is the only solution," they requested a meeting with that organisation. The Heating Employers said they were having discussions with the Master Plumbers. From those discussions, in December 1929 emerged a joint statement by the Employers that in their opinion " some form of Federation is the desirable solution." Accordingly, they invited the two unions to meet and explore the situation on these lines and offered any assistance or co-operation they could give. On the strength of this declaration the U.O.P.A. asked the T.U.C. to try to persuade the Heating Engineers to withdraw their request for arbitration.

To their credit, the Heating Engineers did so. The Executives of the two unions met in February 1930 and recommended that the joint statement of the Employers be endorsed by both memberships and that a Confederation be established with the immediate objects of the control of the industry, the regulation of wages and working conditions and the complete organisation of all operatives employed in the industries embraced by the Confederation. The new body was to have a trial run of four years' duration: in its final year the two unions would meet again to review the position, with the ultimate aim of amalgamating during the ensuing twelve months.

That critical meeting on 5th February, 1930, must have been under the influence of the patron saint of plumbing or his equivalent. Having agreed at last to work together, for at least four years, the delegates went on to establish a basis of demarcation on hot water services for the intervening period. If disputes *did* occur, the work was to be apportioned on a fifty-fifty basis of the total labour value of the contract. Where local disputes committees failed to reach agreement, a Reference Board of national representatives would be the final arbiter.

Such a surfeit of " sweet reason " after so many decades of unmitigated rivalry and frustration could only now be accounted for by those who took part in the 1930 negotiations. Smooth, swift progress continued. The scheme of confederation was endorsed by a special meeting of U.O.P.A. district representatives held in London. The national Reference Committee was set up almost immediately; it consisted of Messrs. C. M. Smeaton and F. A. Norris from the Employers, with John Stephenson and E. Pacey (G.S. of the Heating Engineers' Union) representing the operatives. By the middle of April the main principles of the confederation had been agreed by both Executives and only the details remained to be filled in.

The main principles, and the final Confederation scheme itself, were endorsed by U.O.P.A. members by majorities of about three to one. So, for the first time ever, a degree of amity and common purpose permeated the two operatives' associations and brought a welcome gleam of light into the deepening gloom of the early 'thirties, which would be largely remembered for widespread industrial depression, the " Means Test," the rise of the Nazis and the Jarrow hunger march. The first meeting of the Central Executive of the Confederation took place in London in December 1930 and area committees were being established early in the following year.

Arising from a decision taken at a special N.F.B.T.O. Conference at Chester in October 1930, another attempt was made in 1931 to translate the age-old dream of " one union for the building industry " into reality. Once again, however, the attempt was fruitless. Among the building unions there was still so much preoccupation with the past and so

much reluctance to relinquish vested interests that the outcome was never really in doubt except to the incurable
optimists. As the U.O.P.A. Executive pointed out, the only
logical solution was the amalgamation of *all* the building
unions, and not merely of those who had been mandated by
their members to take part in the scheme. When the final
proposals were submitted to the votes of members of affiliated
unions, only the C.E.U., A.U.B.T.W., Painters and Labourers
could produce favourable majorities.

More useful work was done at the sixteenth Delegate Meeting of the United Operative Plumbers, held at St. Ann's Hall,
Venn Street, Clapham, in May 1931. After previous abortive
attempts, the Association's title was changed for the first
time since its inception in 1865. In preference to a suggestion
from Ireland that the title should be The Amalgamated Society
of Plumbers and Allied Trades, delegates re-christened the
association " The Plumbers, Glaziers and Domestic Engineers
Union." Earlier frustrations on legal procedure were overcome by securing a simple assurance from the Registrar of
Friendly Societies that a vote taken at the D.M. on a membership basis would be sufficient to permit the change of title to
be approved by law.

Faced with what the General Secretary described as " the
very serious financial crisis that is rapidly approaching," delegates took further measures to tighten up the Union's finances
and administrative methods. Responsibility for the audit of
Lodge books and returns was placed firmly in the hands of
General Office. Lodge returns were to be made weekly in
future. The Industrial Table B, for members over 55 years
of age, was introduced and certain modifications were made
to the scale of superannuation payments in order to reduce
the increasing financial demands made by this benefit. The
union's unwavering antagonism to piecework in any shape or
form was diluted slightly by the introduction of a new rule
prohibiting piecework " unless provided for by a national
agreement and authorised by the E.C." (although this
modification was made primarily to meet the situation in the
engineering industry, where plumbers had been committed to
piecework schemes since 1922). Authority was also given to
the Executive to convene conferences of D.C. representatives,

when considered necessary, to discuss particular aspects of Union policy.

Minor amendments to rule introduced practices now firmly embodied in the union's procedures. The E.C. Chairman would preside over future Delegate Meetings: the period of office for full-time District Officials was fixed at five years, nominations were to be confined to members of Lodges within the D.C. area, and the length of candidates' manifestoes limited to 300 words. Delegates still refused, however, to allow more than two members of the E.C. to attend the D.M.

By 1932, with the Means Test in operation, shipbuilding yards nearly idle (average unemployment in Scottish yards in 1931 had risen to 60 per cent of the total labour force) and the British Labour Movement giving full support to the Geneva Disarmament Conference, the P.G. & D.E.U. found itself in further financial difficulties. At the D.M. it had been decided to " write off " the amount of £33,000 borrowed over preceding years from the Reserve Fund to meet current liabilities on the General Fund; since the D.M., however, another £8,500 had been drawn from the reserves to keep pace with rising expenditure, particularly on out-of-work benefit. But the reserves, now reduced to £24,000, were clearly insufficient to meet further anticipated demands for benefit in the light of rising unemployment. Accordingly the E.C. declared that from May 1932 out-of-work benefit would be cut from 10s. to 7s. 6d. a week for Table A members and from 6s. to 4s. 6d. a week for Industrial members.

The Superannuation Fund was another source of worry. In spite of the novel idea of boosting it from the proceeds of a draw on the Manchester November Handicap each year—which yielded pofits of £1,500 in 1931 and £1,120 in 1932—the Fund had a deficit of over £5,000 at the beginning of 1933. Something had to be done quickly. Certain suggestions from the country and the E.C. were put to a vote of the members, who decided to adopt the new scale of payments proposed by the Leeds D.C. (ranging from 6s. to 10s. a week according to length of membership) and at the same time to endorse the Executive's suggestion that this benefit be cut by 25 per cent throughout. As a result, a new scale of superannuation benefit ranging from 4s. 6d. to 7s. 6d. a week became effective in August 1933.

Nor was this the end of the affair. It was only logical, perhaps, that after such drastic reductions had been made in out-of-work and superannuation benefits, sickness benefit should not escape the axe. It, too, was cut by about 20 per cent.

Why were these cuts in benefit accepted by U.O.P.A. members without demur? Only because, at the time, there was no practical alternative to save the Union from foundering. As John Stephenson said: "Most of our members would prefer that benefit should be reduced rather than submit to a further call on their present limited incomes." The economic chaos and dole queues of the hungry 'thirties offered no encouragement to the imposition of higher contributions or national levies.

The privations of those years was reflected in the hesitancy of unions, including the P.G. & D.E.U., to become entangled in major disputes. In the shipbuilding industry in particular there was no hope of national resistance to reactionary measures dictated by the employers. In 1931, cuts of 2s. 6d. a week were made in shipyard workers' wages; the joint Executives of the unions involved " decided to advise members that owing to the present industrial circumstances it was felt we could not successfully resist the reduction." Three years later there was further trouble in the industry when wages of shipyard welders were " brought into conformity " with the national time rate of 60s. for a 47-hour week and trainee welders were introduced by employers into almost every shipbuilding district in spite of strenuous protests from the unions. Once again, however, militant action was out of the question and it was left to districts to offer whatever opposition they could muster.

The life-span of the Confederation set up in 1930 by the four parties involved in the plumbing and heating engineering industry was moving towards its end in 1934. In line with the original undertaking, both of the operatives' Associations submitted to their respective memberships a jointly agreed scheme for the amalgamation of the two organisations. There is no point in examining the merits of the scheme, since when the voting results were published it was found that in spite of overwhelming endorsement by the Plumbers the scheme had been utterly rejected by the operative Heating Engineers, only 400 of whom voted in favour of it in a poll of more than 3,000. Extreme disappointment was expressed at the ensuing four-party conference and in December John Stephenson advised his officials that they should approach local Heating Engineering Employers if fresh difficulties were encountered after the Confederation arrangements were terminated at the end of the year.

Coincident with the death of the four-year truce on heating work came the expiration of John Stephenson's first period of office as General Secretary. He was challenged by a member of Hull Lodge, but in the subsequent ballot was returned to office by a majority of more than ten to one.

On the industrial front the depression had passed its nadir and the immediate future, at least from an economic point of view, looked a little brighter. Wages began to rise again, notably in engineering and building, and the finances of the P.G. & D.E.U. also showed signs of recovery. During 1935 it became possible to restore out-of-work and sickness benefit payments to their correct levels in accordance with rule. George Harris was returned to office as Assistant General Secretary on the first ballot against three opponents, while a former member of the seven-man Executive Council of the 'twenties, E. J. Shea of Cardiff, was appointed National Secretary of the National Registration of Plumbers. Elections were also held for members of the E.C. Fred Hoey and T. McKenna were returned unopposed; their three colleagues (J. W. Pickford, T. McMenemy and P. Walsh) were re-elected. Thus the composition of the Plumbers' Executive remained as it had been for the previous eight years, with four members having served continuously for fifteen years.

During this period there were further disputes between the building craft unions and the " labourers' unions " over recruitment. The Plumbers had already clashed with the N.U.G. & M.W. in the gas industry: late in 1935, the National Union of Public Employees were taken before the T.U.C.

Disputes Committee over their activities in enrolling building craftsmen. The T.U.C. came down heavily in favour of the plaintiffs. " It shall not be the general policy of the National Union of Public Employees," the Disputes Committee stated, " to enrol craftsmen in the building trades in competition with the craft unions. They will thus be in the same position as that voluntarily adopted by the Transport and General Workers' Union and the National Union of General and Municipal Workers, both of which have considerable membership in local government employment."

Blood was now returning fast to the veins of the unions to relieve the anæmic pallor caused by several years of industrial starvation. The end of 1935 saw a nineteen-week dispute in the building industry in what might be considered—even today—as one of the most unlikely areas for demonstrations of trade union unity; the Scottish Highlands. Employers in the Inverness and Dingwall region had refused to accept decisions of the Scottish N.J.C. for the Building Industry but were successfully brought into line by the united efforts of the operatives.

The time was drawing near for another Delegate Meeting of the P.G. & D.E.U.—the seventeenth. Familiar names appeared on the Standing Orders Committee; Belfast stalwart G. M. Donaldson, George Alton of London (later to become a National Trustee), T. R. McDonald of Glasgow, T. Ortton of Newcastle and D. K. Walker of Birmingham. Fred Hoey presided over the D.M., held again at St. Ann's Hall in Venn Street in May 1936. Possibly one of the most important steps taken was the decision to rejoin the Engineering and Shipbuilding Trades' Federation, from which the U.O.P.A. had resigned in 1922 after fruitless efforts to secure a modernisation of the Federation's policies and machinery, when the Plumbers had joined other disillusioned craft unions in a separate Craft Unions' Committee. In 1935 the F.E.S.T. had undergone a major overhaul and had been given a new constitution, in the drafting of which John Stephenson and T. McKenna had played prominent parts. There was unanimous agreement that the P.G. & D.E.U. should affiliate to the modernised organisation, to be known as the Confederation of Shipbuilding and Engineering Unions.

Delegates also withdrew their previous objections to the attendance at Delegate Meetings of all members of the E.C., but there was scant support for a suggestion from Northern Ireland that the union should revert to the old practice of government by a part-time Executive; even with the support of London delegates the proposal was defeated by 50 votes to 7. In fact, the permanence of the E.C. was strengthened by the extension of their period of office from three years to five, bringing them into line with full-time district officials.

Further modifications were made to the Union's administration. Lodge financial procedure was amended to provide for the proper banking of cash in hand and for advances to be made to Lodges by General Office on request. The E.C. was authorised to invest up to 75 per cent of the Reserve Fund in Trustee Securities, the interest to be allocated to the superannuation fund. Contributions were in future to be taken as flat-rate payments (apart from local levies) from which all benefit expenditure would be met. Thus the ancient system of multifarious pigeon-holes for this fund and that, like a series of separate " piggy-banks," was almost abolished. With the upturn in industrial activity, it is not surprising that the craft contribution was raised by 4d. a week to 1s. 9d. Strike benefit was maintained at £1 a week, but a new benefit was added to the rules: Victimisation Benefit. The payment would be £2 a week. It was also decided that the P.G. & D.E.U. should publish its own journal every quarter, although the first issue did not actually appear until eleven years later.

The Union's financial prospects were certainly more cheerful than for many years, but the razor's edge on which it had balanced so precariously since the previous D.M. became apparent when it was revealed to delegates that no less than 90.1 per cent of all contributions collected during the previous five years had been paid out again in benefits.

The E.C. were instructed to give special consideration to the problems of organisation, and the expenditure involved was to be a charge on the Reserve Fund. Consequently in September 1936 the Executive decided to appoint the first full-time Organisers, although limiting their service initially to a period of twelve months. From this decision sprang later

EXECUTIVE COUNCIL AND GENERAL OFFICERS, 1952

D. Fraser, T. R. McDonald, C. McMullan, Alex Johnson, G. H. Morgan,
Geo. H. Harris (A.G.S.), Hugh Kelly (G.S.), A. E. Soones (A.G.S.)

HUGH KELLY, O.B.E.
General Secretary, 1965

developments which culminated in the establishment of National Organisers as full-time officers of the Union.

Not long before the D.M. assembled, the E.C. had been successful in drawing up an agreement with the Heating Engineering Employers to cover P.G. & D.E.U. members working in the industry. There had been an urgent need for some kind of agreement to fill the vacuum created by the termination of the Confederation scheme and subsequent failure of the two operatives' organisations to achieve amalgamation. The Plumbing Employers also agreed to join in the new arrangements, which thus became a " three-party " agreement. At the Delegate Meeting the E.C. were complimented on having made a substantial contribution to the solution of the Union's problems in this field and at the same time having improved the position of all the operatives concerned. The agreement, John Stephenson said, " has set aside for all time the idea that the members of this organisation are only temporarily associated with the Heating and Ventilating Industry, and increasing numbers are securing employment."

At the 1936 meeting, delegates also endorsed the first of a number of separate agreements which were to be reached by the P.G. & D.E.U. and certain employers' associations. This was the Patent Glazing Agreement, negotiated with the Engineering Employers' Federation, which preserved building trade rates for plumbers working on patent glazing: it was effective from July 1936. In February the following year, the Plumbers set their seal on a similar agreement with the Association of Roofing Felt Employers; there was a long standing arrangement already existing with the Ruberoid Company, but when this firm combined with others to form the Employers' Association the need arose for a new agreement.

A conference of representatives of London Lodges and the District Committee was held in April 1937, when the problems of organisation in the Metropolitan area were closely examined. As a result of the discussions some readjustment was made to the structure and operation of the D.C. and its jurisdiction was confined to an area with an outer limit of 17 miles from Charing Cross.

L

Despite the general revival of trade and fortune which marked the beginning of the " Munich " period, the year 1937 produced a bitter dispute in Eire. Cork building trade employers had offered a wage increase of 1½d. an hour to all craftsmen except plumbers, who were expected to be satisfied with an hourly rise of a halfpenny because they already enjoyed a higher rate than their fellow craftsmen. The conflict continued for ten weary months, but the determination of Cork members of the P.G. & D.E.U. never wavered. In February 1938 the Lodge earned the congratulations of the Executive for having finally achieved a satisfactory settlement.

In the early months of Europe's final year of peace it was found necessary to call a special Delegate Meeting. The Executive Council had been in conflict with certain Lodges over the interpretation of rules and payment of benefit without E.C. authorisation. When delegates met at St. Ann's Hall on 31st May the Chairman, T. McMenemy, explained that " various Lodges have claimed the right to interpret a rule while keeping to the letter of that rule. Chaos tended to spread." Further confusion had arisen over the Union's affiliation to joint councils, federations and other industrial groupings. " A delicate position emerged in a legal sense," said the Chairman, " because of the vested interests of the members in the property of the Union. There was the possibility of the Union becoming involved in actions which might have been harmful to the prestige, dignity and integrity of the Union." During the proceedings John Stephenson revealed that serious difficulties had arisen when one member had refused to accept the decisions of industrial conciliation machinery, which had been invoked on his behalf. Such a situation obviously needed to be clarified. Accordingly, the appropriate amendments to rule were approved by delegates to the special D.M. to ensure that commitments entered into by the Union itself were binding upon all its members.

But the special D.M. did much more than simply confirm the authority of the association over its members. It introduced one of the keystones of the Union's modern structure—the Final Appeal Court. This was to be a body comprising five lay members of the P.G. & D.E.U. who would meet annually to consider appeals from individual members against decisions imposed upon them. This power had always rested previously in the Delegate Meeting, but the five-year interval between one D.M. and the next was reason enough for the establishment of an alternative form of appeals machinery. Delegates also gave the Executive authority to expel members who refused to conform to the Union's rules or whose actions brought injury or discredit to the P.G. & D.E.U.

Members of the first Final Appeal Court, elected in the same year, were H. W. Newman of London No. 1, T. H. Cartledge of Liverpool, T. Ortton of Newcastle, T. R. McDonald of Glasgow and C. McMullan of Belfast.

By 1939 the true intentions of Hitler and his henchmen had become crystal clear to even the staunchest supporters of Neville Chamberlain and his policy of appeasement. After less than twenty years of precarious peace, Europe found itself plunged once again into a bloodbath. The effects of the Second World War on British trade unions were in many respects similar to those of the earlier catastrophe. As the ordinary citizen had to sacrifice many treasured personal liberties, so did the trade union member have to relinquish many of his traditional rights as a member of an industrial organisation. Such restrictions are inescapable in time of war. Dilution, for example, became accepted in many industries in which the supply of skilled craft labour was inadequate. Established customs, protection earned slowly and with great difficulty by the trade union pioneers, vested interests in certain craft operations—all were put aside for the sake of national survival: and, indeed, it cannot be gainsaid that in 1940 Britain came closer to defeat and occupation by a foreign power than at any time since the Battle of Hastings.

Two particular domestic events in the affairs of the P.G. & D.E.U. occurred during the first years of the war. Since 1936 the "three-party agreement" on heating work had continued in operation, but towards the end of 1939 the two Employers' Associations had indicated a strong desire for a return to the four-party arrangements that had worked so well in the 'thirties. The Plumbers, however, insisted that

L1

the entry of the Heating Engineers' Union to any new four-party scheme should be conditional upon their recognition of the 1936 agreement. The Heating Engineers accepted this, and accordingly a new Four-Party Agreement became operative on 6th February, 1940, covering wages and working conditions of *all* craftsmen engaged in the heating and ventilating industry. Further progress was made a year later when the two operatives' associations reached agreement on the mutual recognition of cards where, because of war-time labour shortages, either party was unable to supply the required number of craftsmen on any particular contract. Both parties had already declared that they would not " poach " each other's members during the period of the war.

As a negotiator, John Stephenson had earned widespread respect on the British industrial scene. Early in 1940 he was approached by the Minister of Labour and asked to place his industrial knowledge and experience at the disposal of the Government for the duration. With the consent of his E.C., the Plumbers' General Secretary accepted the invitation on the understanding that he would not have to give up his leadership of the Union or his position as Chairman of the Confederation of S. & E. Unions.

During the war the first changes for many years occurred in the composition of the Executive Council. The member for E.C.1 Division, J. W. Pickford, died suddenly on his way to G.O. in January 1940 and was succeeded by H. W. Newman of London No. 1   Two years later followed the death of the E.C. Officer for the North-East, T. McKenna; his place was taken by George Morgan of Sunderland,   Meanwhile, both John Stephenson and George Harris had been re-elected. as General Officers for another six years.

In the immediate pre-war years recognition had at last been established, in the form of Parliamentary Legislation, that industrial workers were entitled to an annual holiday with pay. Among the first to make provision on these lines in their industrial agreements were the engineering and shipbuilding industries. One of the last to do so was the building industry, in which it must be admitted there were special difficulties arising from the high degree of movement and " casualisation " within the labour force. Nevertheless these problems were finally overcome, and in February 1943 came the introduction of the Holidays with Pay Scheme, operating on the now familiar stamped card principle.

British industry was now working at full stretch to try to keep pace with the insatiable appetite of the war machine. The interminable production of tanks, guns, aeroplanes and ships made the industrial worker a key figure in the conflict and involved the trade unions in many problems. Piecework systems became commonplace. Even so, the Plumbers repeated their inherent opposition to such forms of wage payment when a vote was taken in 1943 on the proposed suspension of the " piecework rule " for the remaining years of war. The proposal was rejected, but the vote was almost low enough to be inconsequential. John Stephenson pointed out that although the E.C. were also opposed to piecework, the urgent needs of the armed forces must be met. In any case the Plumbers were committed by their 1922 agreement with the Employers to accept bonus schemes in the engineering industry; the Royal Dockyards had operated piecework for many years, and it had been introduced into the building industry under the Essential Work Order. It was the Executive's opinion, said the G.S., that collective schemes of bonus payments were the least objectionable and they were prepared to agree to the participation of P.G. & D.E.U. members in such schemes, subject to prior E.C. examination and approval.

Acting on the authority given at the 1931 D.M., the Executive convened a national conference at Swinton House, Grays Inn Road, in 1943. Representation was on the same basis as for a D.M. It was a welcome opportunity for delegates to exchange views on the various developments in the industries in which plumbers were employed. Certainly there could be little cause for complaint at any delay in " maintaining and improving the conditions of the working lives " of P.G. & D.E.U. members. Holidays with pay, agreements for members in the Royal Ordnance Factories, the chemical industry, the roofing felt industry and the patent glazing industry, a " guaranteed week " agreement for building trade members—all these advances had been made within recent years.   In addition the P.G. & D.E.U. had entered into another " independent " agreement, this time with a group of plumbing employers, to cover rates and conditions of leadburners employed by chemical contractors, and a few months later were to establish, with the Glazing Employers, the National Joint Council for the Glazing Industry. During the discussions at Swinton House, John Stephenson forecast profound changes in materials and techniques of the plumbing crafts-man in the immediate post-war period; two developments he envisaged were the fabrication of complete plumbing units and the widespread introduction of plastics materials.

During 1943 the Union decided to affiliate to the National Council of Labour Colleges and provide free educational facilities for all members.   During the lifetime of the N.C.L.C., whose functions were taken over by the T.U.C. in 1964, many hundreds of members have increased their knowledge on a wide variety of subjects through the correspondence courses and the annual Summer Schools.

Only a few months before victory in Europe the death occurred of Fred Hoey, E.C. Officer for the North-West since 1920.   The ensuing election attracted four candidates, from whom the members ultimately chose Hugh Kelly, secretary of Birkenhead No. 1 Lodge.   This election also drew some critical comment from the Scrutineers, who pointed to the very low return on the first ballot and also to " the apparent method adopted by some Lodges where one individual has cast all the votes.   We think the whole question of ballots should be earnestly considered by Lodges with an eye to the coming D.M."   By the summer of 1945, nominations were being invited for the other four Executive positions.   George Morgan was returned unopposed, while H. W. Newman and T. McMenemy were re-elected on the first ballot.   The only change was in the Irish Division, where the retiring E.C. Officer, Paddy Walsh, was replaced by Charles McMullan of Belfast.

CHAPTER X

CONSOLIDATION AND MODERNISATION

BRITISH unions emerged into the first year of peace with the common determination that the benefits and advances gained during the war should be firmly embodied into a new social order from which mass unemployment and poverty would be abolished for ever. Their resolution was encouraged by strong indications that the legislature were equally determined that the people of Britain should be given a new deal, particularly in the form of improved social welfare services foreshadowed by the Beveridge Committee's report of 1944. Fortunately, the end of hostilities coincided with the election of the first majority Labour Government pledged to give prompt effect to the introduction of social reforms and plans for the public ownership of Britain's key industries and services.

Many of the Labour Government's reforms had already appeared on the Statute Book when the eighteenth and final Delegate Meeting of the P.G. & D.E.U. was held at Maritime House (headquarters of the National Union of Seamen) in Clapham at the end of May 1946. "As a Union," said the Chairman, T. McMenemy, "we have always been making claims for our right to be in the forefront of events. The possibility of being accorded that right may be here at this moment, and we can either accept the opportunity or throw it away."

The 1946 D.M. was undoubtedly critical in the development of the Union, comparable with the one at Jesmond Dene after the First World War when so many major alterations had been made. The Union was now in an almost unassailable position, both numerically and financially. This was underlined by John Stephenson in his financial returns for the ten years since the 1936 Delegate Meeting. From 1931 to 1935 the Union's balances had increased by £1,900: in the ten years 1935-1945, they had risen by no less than £252,000. Since the end of 1935 membership had nearly doubled, from 24,730 to 41,200.

One of the most important results of the 1946 discussions

was a complete reorganisation of the Union's regional structure. District boundaries were revised, eventually reducing the number of districts from 34 to 28, and nearly all of them were to have a full-time District Secretary, whose salary and expenses would be a charge on the General Funds of the Union. Formerly, the cost of full-time District Officials had been met to some extent by local levies. Thus the P.G. & D.E.U. reached the final stage in the gradual transition of their district administration from the old voluntary basis to a professional level in keeping with the needs of the times.

The 1946 Delegate Meeting also signed its own death warrant. Over the years, and with rapid acceleration during the Second World War, the Union's business had become more and more complex; its influence extended into an increasing number of industries and a widening range of negotiating machinery. Moreover, with the advent of a strong Labour Government and the obvious corollary of closer and continuous liaison between Government Departments and trade unions, the original functions and frequency of the Delegate Meeting were no longer adequate. Delegates accordingly accepted the proposal that the Union's future national assemblies should be on a dual basis, one conference dealing solely with Union policy and the other confined to the revision of the rules. The Biennial Conference and the Rules Revision Committee were born. Representation at the biennial policy conference would be similar to that laid down for the D.M., while attendance at the Rules Revision Committee would be limited to two delegates from each District.

Yet another anachronism was removed in 1946 with the abolition of the system of electing full-time officials by votes of members taken at Lodge meetings. The Lodge vote remained available for questions of policy, but future elections of officials were to to be determined by an individual ballot in which every member of the Union received a ballot paper by post, returnable to G.O. or the District Office according to the requirements of the election.

Contributions were increased by 3d. a week: Lodge management was simplified, uniform pence cards were introduced and provision was made for every member to receive a quarterly statement of account. In view of the heavy burden of administrative work at G.O. it was decided that a second A.G.S. should be elected.

Finally, delegates made one other critical decision which compensated for previous frustrations. There could be no longer any doubt that the trade unions were irrevocably welded to the Parliamentary Labour Party and vice versa. Plumbers now accepted this fact and unanimously agreed that the Union should take the necessary steps to establish its own political fund and should affiliate to the Labour Party.

With the increasing trend towards the employment of a full-time " general staff " it was also recognised that such employment should offer the same degree of security as that obtaining in outside industry. The Executive Council was therefore given authority to establish a superannuation fund for the full-time officials and clerical staff in the Union's service.

The 1946 D.M. also changed the Union's title. The United Operative Plumbers' Association of Great Britain and Ireland, which had become The Plumbers, Glaziers and Domestic Engineers' Union in 1931, was now further abbreviated to the Plumbing Trades' Union.

Shortly the D.M. had ended there was an upheaval in the trade union movement in the Irish Republic when a number of unions broke away from the Irish T.U.C. and formed a rival body known as the Congress of Irish Unions. This organisation received official recognition from the Eire Government. Arising from discussions at a conference convened by the British T.U.C., the Executive Council asked Lodges in Eire to declare whether they wished to remain with the P.T.U. (which was affiliated to the Irish T.U.C.) or wanted to leave the Union and set up a separate society of plumbers in order to throw in their lot with the C.I.U. It must have given the E.C. a good deal of satisfaction when they were able to report to the T.U.C. some time later that the plumbers in the Irish Republic stood solidly beside their colleagues in Britain.

By the summer of 1947 the election of an additional A.G.S. was completed. The new officer at G.O. was the former

London District Secretary, A. E. Soones, who defeated T. R. McDonald of Glasgow in the third ballot. The recruiting capacity of the P.T.U. was strengthened by the appointment by the E.C. of three National Organisers—S. T. Buttery (later to become E.C. Officer for Division 3), F. H. Curran and J. H. Harley.

With the Labour Government's nationalisation of transport and other public services, the counsel of John Stephenson was very much in demand in various Ministries. His war-time contributions as Labour Adviser to the Board of Trade and the Ministry of Aircraft Production had been recognised by the award of a C.B.E.; at the beginning of 1948 he received a knighthood. At the end of that year his career reached its peak; he was invited to become Chairman of the Eastern Gas Board when the gas industry was transferred to public owner-ship in April 1949. He accepted, relinquishing his leadership of the P.T.U. " with a membership more than doubled during my term of office and the finances strong enough to meet any future needs." To his new appointment he promised to carry the ideals of the trade union movement, from which the public ownership of industry had sprung. " We must meet the chal-lenge that it brings," he concluded, " by accepting, in shop or board room, the responsibilities of this change in control."

A formidable list of candidates appeared on the first ballot paper for Sir John Stephenson's successor. Among them were the A.G.S., A. E. Soones, C. C. Brownlie (who has been N.F.B.T.O. Scottish Regional Secretary for many years), Executive Officers Hugh Kelly and George Morgan, T. R. McDonald, T. W. Sullivan (London District Secretary), E. Corrigan from Newcastle and D. K. Walker of Birmingham. After the election had gone to a third ballot, Hugh Kelly of Birkenhead was victorious over his E.C. colleague G. H. Morgan, and moved into General Office in February 1950.

With one obvious exception at the beginning of the twentieth century, the Plumbers have been extremely fortunate (or wise, perhaps) in their choice of General Secretaries. George Cherry, J. H. Edmiston, Lachlan MacDonald, John Stephenson and Hugh Kelly have all brought to the Union's highest office a wide experience, complete integrity and devotion to duty. Being human, they have been fallible: but with each one the first priority has been the welfare of the Union and its members.

In the year preceding Sir John Stephenson's departure the P.T.U. held the first of the new biennial policy conferences at Edinburgh. Since then there have been eight others, at various centres throughout the length and breadth of the British Isles, and the tenth Biennial Conference will be assembling at Eastbourne in May 1966. The opinion has sometimes been expressed that this conference should be abolished, mainly on grounds of expense. There have also been attempts to make it an annual event. However, it seems to be firmly established in its present form as a permanent feature of the Union's machinery. So, too, is the Rules Revision Committee, meeting at six-year intervals (normally at Maritime House) to revise the Union's rule book.

Events of the past fifteen years are too fresh in the minds of P.T.U. members to justify the detailed account we have given of the Union's progress in earlier times. The Plumbers have continued to consolidate their position and modernise their rules, administration and policies. At the first meeting of the R.R.C. in 1951, for example, the Superannuation Benefit Fund was abolished and the Union's remaining obligations to eligible members of Table A (closed to new entrants at the same meeting and replaced by the General Table) were declared to be a liability on the General Fund of the Union. The last remnants of the " craft pride " of Victorian plumbers, which however sincere in those days did undoubtedly encourage the inauguration and growth of the Heating Engineers' Union and the subsequent squabbles with the plumbers, were swept aside by a decision to accept into the P.T.U. plumbers' labourers (" mates " or " assistants "), for whom the Auxiliary Table was set up. The employment of National Organisers, previously appointed by the Executive Council at their discretion, was given proper recognition in the rules, with the proviso that one of them should be a glazier and that they should all be elected by ballot vote in the same way as other full-time officials. The 1951 R.R.C.

also decided that one A.G.S. was sufficient; when George Harris retired in the following year the vacancy was accordingly left unfilled.

Hugh Kelly's report to his first R.R.C. meeting revealed the substantial progress made by the Union since the end of the war. Membership, standing at 41,000 at the end of 1945, had risen to 54,500 by the end of 1950. For the first time ever the Union's balance had topped the £500,000 mark, of which £376,000 was held in the Reserve Fund. This was indeed a far cry from the poverty-stricken years of the 'twenties and 'thirties when the Union's survival was very much in doubt.

Appearing with monotonous regularity on the agendas of Biennial Conferences since 1948 has been the issue of amalgamation with the Heating Engineers' Union. Fresh discussions took place in 1950 and a sub-committee of the two Executives was instructed to give detailed consideration to ways and means of achieving the ultimate solution to inter-union strife. Once again, as in the 'thirties, progress was made to the point of submitting concrete amalgamation proposals to a vote of the members of both unions. The result, published early in 1953, was "the mixture as before." Plumbers voted wholeheartedly in favour of the merger, although the total poll of 12,500 was very disappointing. However, this fact was irrelevant in the face of a substantial anti-amalgamation vote from the other union. Further progress was rendered well-nigh impossible by two formidable obstacles: the understandable insistence of the Plumbers that the superannuation rights of P.T.U. members must be guaranteed under any joint agreement, and the repeated demand of the Heating Engineers for a " recognition of cards " and equal rights to carry out work on domestic water supplies.

In utter frustration the P.T.U. Executive turned to the members later in 1953 and asked for a reappraisal of the Union's position under the Four-Party Agreement, which had functioned since 1940 and laid down rates and conditions for operatives employed in the heating and ventilating industry. The E.C. declared that in their opinion it was time for the Plumbers to withdraw from the agreement " and so leave ourselves free to fight the issue of domestic supplies without

A. E. SOONES, Assistant General Secretary, 1965

Members of the Executive Council, 1965

Bro. D. Fraser   E.C. 1

Bro. F. McGuffie   E.C. 2

Bro. C. Lovell   E.C. 3

Bro. H. T. Barrett   E.C. 4

Bro. J. Scott   E.C. 5

having to go through the conciliation procedure. It must, however, be clearly understood that if the agreement is terminated we stand to lose the additional rates paid to our members under the Four-Party arrangements. In cases of dispute we would then be claiming that domestic supplies are exclusively a plumbing trade operation and as such should come under building trade rates and conditions."

Despite an apathetic vote, totalling about 3,100, the verdict of the members endorsed the Executive's opinion. Action was deferred, however, until a full discussion could take place at the 1954 Biennial Conference at Blackpool. The debate was followed by overwhelming assent that the P.T.U. should withdraw from the Four-Party Agreement.

The wisdom of this decision has since been the subject of much argument and further discussion at conferences. Some feel it was too precipitous, taken as it was in an atmosphere of frustration created by yet another impasse with the Heating Engineers' Union. Others argue that the Agreement had for years been more a hindrance than a help to the Plumbers in their legitimate attempts to safeguard their work against incursions by heating engineers. Wherever the truth may lie, the fact remains that in the ten years since the 1954 decision there has been no appreciable progress towards the goal of amalgamation. Further discussions at Executive level have been little more, in the final analysis, than an academic exercise—particularly in the light of a recent decision by the Heating Engineers' triennial conference that a merger with the P.T.U. was not to be pursued. The Plumbers, on the other hand, have turned to other unions with similar interests in the search for closer unity: progress has been promising.

Two more meetings of the Rules Revision Committee, in 1957 and 1963, brought further additions and modifications to the P.T.U. General Rules. In 1957 all full-time officials of the Union were made fully mobile by the provision of cars, in line with the practice of modern business organisations. Such a move would surely have been received with horror in earlier years, but it is an indication that the P.T.U. was deter-

M

mined to move with the times and give their negotiators the
" tools for the job." Another innovation designed to speed
up the administration of the Union was the substitution of
monthly meetings of the Executive Council for the old
quarterly ones. Pressure of Union business on the E.C. had
gradually increased the duration of their quarterly meetings
to nearly a fortnight, and there were two other serious disadvantages: the long interval between meetings, during which
many important issues needing an E.C. decision had to be
held in abeyance, and the necessity for the Executive Officer
to be away from his area (and his family) for two weeks at
a time.

Certain changes were also made to the rules governing the
election of full-time officials. Executive Officers, previously
elected by a national vote, were in future to be elected by
ballot of the members in their own division. At the same
time, the election procedure was standardised for all full-time
positions.

An important addition to the rules made in 1957 gave legal
endorsement to the National Distress Fund. This was inaugurated four years earlier by the E.C. as a result of a Lodge
vote endorsing their action in making emergency grants from
General Funds to relieve hardship and financial embarrass-
ment suffered by members whose homes and property had
been affected by the East Coast flood disaster early in 1953.
When the Lodge vote was taken, P.T.U. members endorsed
not only the Executive's emergency action but also the proposal that a special levy should be imposed on all members
for the purpose of setting up a " Distress Fund " for future
emergencies. Since then, of course, the Fund has taken its
place in the rule book and is now financed by an annual levy
of 1s. per member. However streamlined it may become, the
modern trade union should never lose sight of this original
precept of the early trade unionists—the resolve to give a
helping hand to their less fortunate comrades.

In the light of later events elsewhere in the British trade
union movement, it is interesting to note that the final item
of business at the 1957 R.R.C. was an attempt to disqualify
members of " proscribed organisations " from holding any
full-time, paid office in the Plumbing Trades Union. Need-

less to say, the proposed new rule invoked passionate arguments, but it was firmly rejected by 32 votes to 17.

Six years later the Rules Revision Committee reassembled at Maritime House for the conference which produced the Union's current General Rules. No world-shattering decisions emerged and no drastic alterations were made to the structure of the P.T.U. There were, to be sure, some noteworthy innovations. Delegates from East Anglia successfully introduced a proposal that Union contributions should fluctuate with movements in building trade basic wage rates. If there was a penny an hour increase in wages, there should be a penny a week rise in contributions. The general problems of finance were dealt with at length by the General Secretary, who underlined the fact that for several years the Union's expenditure had exceeded the amount collected in contributions. This situation was obviously undesirable, although there could be no comparison with the critical years of the 'twenties and 'thirties when the Union hovered on the brink of oblivion. Hugh Kelly's warnings, however, were taken to heart: such increases as were made at the 1963 R.R.C. to benefits and other payments were quite small, and many amendments met defeat apparently by virtue of their financial implications. Such a one was the attempt to extend " professionalism " in the Union by authorising the election of more full-time Lodge Secretaries, at the discretion of the E.C., to operate on much the same basis as District Secretaries. The proposal was rejected by only a narrow margin.

Divided opinion was again revealed on the merits of national or divisional elections. A move to revert to the former practice of electing Executive Officers by national ballot was defeated, but on the other hand the rule governing the election of the members of the Standing Orders Committee was amended in the opposite direction, putting future elections on a divisional instead of a national basis.

A survivor from the past which gave rise to much controversy over the years—the " piecework rule "—was removed altogether and replaced by a short, new section which states, quite simply, that only those Payment-by-Results systems which are based on national or district agreements can be recognised and operated by P.T.U. members. It is worth remembering that less than fifty years ago plumbers were liable to fines of five shillings a day for having any truck with piecework.

In the course of time the rule governing the conduct of disputes and payment of strike benefit had grown extremely cumbersome and complex. In 1963, Hugh Kelly scored a minor triumph by persuading delegates to accept, *in toto*, a completely revised strike rule which he had drafted himself. By the time the R.R.C. meets again in 1969 the Union will be under a new leader; and so, as Lachlan MacDonald did in his own day, Hugh Kelly has left his personal mark on the rules of the Union.

On paper, a union's financial problems may be solved by a small increase in the weekly contribution. With the decline in recent times in the numbers of active trade unionists, that is to say those who attend branch meetings and are not merely apathetic card-carriers, it has become correspondingly more difficult to obtain the voluntary Lodge officers without whose loyalty and service the Union could not function under its existing constitution. Automatic adjustment of contributions in step with wage increases does to some extent remove the financial anxieties which could develop, often acutely, in the interval between rules revision conferences; nevertheless, the critical problem nowadays is the actual collection of money from the members. Delegates at Maritime House in 1963 went part of the way towards overcoming this difficulty by accepting a suggestion that " contribution collectors " should be appointed where necessary and would receive a commission of 1s. in the pound on the amount they collected. At present it is still too early to assess the real value of this innovation.

*   *   *

What of the future? In the foreword to this history we declared our intention not to make prophesies. No crystal ball is required, however, to see the growing recognition by British trade unions of the urgent need to move closer together, to eliminate the dead wood, to streamline the

machinery and to face the fact that one of their original functions—the provision of "friendly" benefits—is rapidly
becoming obsolete. No government, however reactionary,
could ever hope to survive if it attempted partially or wholly
to destroy the social services which were established in this
country after the Second World War. It is only logical, therefore, that the modern trade union, while striving to its utmost
by means of its links with the Labour Party to preserve beneficial legislation, should devote more and more of its energies
and finances to the second original function: the improvement of the wages and working conditions of its members.

Thus we must acknowledge the possibility that within the
next decade the Plumbing Trades Union will surrender its
individuality in the cause of the general progress of the
wider movement. Should this come to pass, it will be sad for
those members who still remember the days of hardship and
sacrifice, when their membership of the Union was both
hazardous and something to be proud of. But it will be even
sadder for future generations of craftsmen whose forebears
once worked only with lead if the opportunity, when it
becomes ripe, is overlooked because of lack of vision or
declined for selfish motives. The truth of the remark that
" there are too many unions and not enough trade unionists "
becomes more acutely obvious as each year passes. The
future trend must inevitably be towards unification.

Wherever the road ahead may lead, one thing can be said
with certainty. Man will never live without water: while
there is water, there will be plumbers. And you may be sure,
brothers, that so long as there are plumbers—there will be
plumbers in unity.

GENERAL SECRETARIES

JOSEPH H. DOBB (LIVERPOOL)	1865-1868
GEORGE MAY (LIVERPOOL)	1868-1876
WM. J. BARNETT (NOTTINGHAM)	1876-1879
GEORGE BAKER CHERRY (HULL)	1879-1902
EDWARD ELLIS BURNS (GLASGOW NO. 1) ...	1902-1909
JOHN H. EDMISTON (MANCHESTER NO. 2) ...	1910-1919
LACHLAN MACDONALD (GLASGOW NO. 2) ...	1919-1929
JOHN WALKER STEPHENSON (NEWCASTLE UPON TYNE)	1929-1949
HUGH KELLY (BIRKENHEAD NO. 1)	1950 to date

*   *   *

ASSISTANT GENERAL SECRETARIES

T. H. CHERRY	1896-1910
LACHLAN MACDONALD	1911-1919
J. L. SMYTH	1919-1928
JOHN W. STEPHENSON	1928-1929
GEORGE H. HARRIS	1929-1952
A. E. SOONES	1947 to date

MEMBERS OF THE
FULL-TIME EXECUTIVE COUNCIL
1920 *to date*

DIVISION No. 1 (Southern England and South Wales)

J. W. PICKFORD (BRISTOL)	1920-1940
H. W. NEWMAN (LONDON NO. 1)	1940-1949
D. FRASER (BARNES)	1950-

DIVISION No. 2 (North-Western England)

F. HOEY (LIVERPOOL NO. 1)	1920-1945
HUGH KELLY (BIRKENHEAD NO. 1)	1945-1950
ALEX JOHNSON (BIRKENHEAD NO. 2)	1950-1957
F. McGUFFIE (BIRKENHEAD NO. 1)	1957-

DIVISION No. 3 (North-Eastern England)

T. MCKENNA (NEWCASTLE-UPON-TYNE)	1920-1942
G. H. MORGAN (SUNDERLAND)	1942-1953
S. T. BUTTERY (LINCOLN)	1954-1963
C. LOVELL (WALLSEND)	1963-

DIVISION No. 4 (Scotland)

T. MCMENEMY (GLASGOW GOVAN)	1920-1951
T. R. MCDONALD (GLASGOW GOVAN)	1951-1957
J. C. PATERSON (PAISLEY)	1957-1963
H. T. BARRETT (EDINBURGH)	1964-

DIVISION No. 5 (Ireland)

J. WALKER (BELFAST)	1920-1923
P. WALSH (DUBLIN)	1924-1945
C. MCMULLAN (BELFAST)	1946-1957
J. SCOTT (BELFAST)	1957-

Other members of the Executive Council, before the reduction of the E.C. Divisions from seven to five, were:—

North Scotland

C. R. WORLING (ABERDEEN) **1920-1926**

Wales

E. J. SHEA (CARDIFF) **1920-1926**

DELEGATE MEETINGS

Inaugural Meeting: Liverpool, 27th December, 1865.

1867	Manchester	1905	Manchester
1868	Glasgow	1911	London
1870	Dublin	1919	Newcastle upon Tyne
1873	Edinburgh	1923	London
1876	Nottingham	1926	London
1880	Hull	1931	London
1883	Birmingham	1936	London
1888	Sheffield	1938	London
1891	Leicester		(Emergency)
1895	Liverpool	1946	London

BIENNIAL CONFERENCES

1948	Edinburgh
1950	Dublin
1952	Nottingham
1954	Blackpool
1956	Brighton
1958	Bangor, N.I.
1960	Dunoon
1962	Whitley Bay
1964	New Brighton

MEMBERSHIP (1866-1964)

(End of)

1866	....	1,467
1870	....	1,230
1875	....	1,889
1880	....	2,077
1885	....	2,691
1890	....	5,099
1895	....	8,146
1900	....	11,186
1905	....	11,419
1910	....	10,907
1915	....	12,644
1920	....	25,218
1925	....	23,864
1930	....	24,809
1935	....	24,730
1940	....	34,176
1945	....	41,119
1950	....	54,502
1955	....	56,247
1960	....	54,631
1965 (June)	....	55,086

OPERATIVE PLUMBERS AND GLAZIERS ASSOCIATION

PREFACE TO MINUTE BOOK, 1852

A Society of Operative Plumbers and Glaziers has been in existence in Manchester for upwards of half a Century under various arrangements and has been productive of great benefit to its members and to the operatives in the trade generally in providing in case of sickness, accident or death, to those of its members that have been so unfortunate as to require assistance, and likewise in reducing the hours of labour from eight to ten hours per week and advancing the wages from six to eight shillings per week.

The Society during that period has been both rich and poor, its funds varying from £160 to as many pence, and the number of its members varying in the same proportion. Of late years it has had a deal to contend with particularly in the year 1846 when a formidable combination took place with the employers in the Building Trades, their object being to break up this and all other Trade Societies in the Building Trade. To resist such a combination every effort was made and the Operative Plumbers and Glaziers Society of Manchester expended all its funds and borrowed a considerable sum from its Treasurer. Unfortunately its members for various reasons unexplained left and the Society became merely a name. The Employers took advantage of this and brought out a new code of working rules which would tend materially to increase the hours of labour. During this time a second society was established one for the support of sickness accident and death but did not interfere with the Trade Rules and as the new code of Rules adopted by the Employers interfered with their members as well as the old Society, a meeting was verbally called at the Black Moors Head, Hunts Bank, Manchester, 3rd November, 1851, to take into consideration what steps should be adopted. The meeting was attended by members of both Societies and non-Society men.

The meeting came to the conclusion that the only means for the withdrawal of such obnoxious Rules was the uniting of the two Societies and reorganisation of the Operatives in

Manchester, Salford and vicinities. A copy of the resolution of that meeting was sent to each Society and a committee of eight, four from each Society, was formed to take into consideration the best means of such a reorganisation. And the Committee came to the conclusion that a fund should be set apart by each Society for the support of the members of either Society should they be thrown out of employment for standing up for the defence of the established Rules of the Trade and that a code of Rules should be made for the regulation of the same. The report of that committee being laid before the two Societies, it met their views and a second committee was appointed to draw up a code of Rules so that the two Societies should work in harmony. The second committee consisted of the following persons, viz., from the Black Moors Head Society, Messrs. James Taylor, William Polding, Charles English and Peter Hooley; from the Peter Street Society, Messrs. John Berry, Joshua Sidebottam, James Bell and John Smith. This committee met at the Black Moors Head, 19th December, 1851. After discussing the question of equalising the expenses in trade disputes and how the two Societies could work together in harmony, they came to the conclusion that not only should the expenses of trade disputes be equalised, but that the expenses of sickness, accident and death should also be equalised, and appointed James Taylor to draw up a code of Rules or principles upon which such objects could be carried out and that the same to be submitted to the committee on their next meeting.

The committee met again on the 23rd December, 1851, when James Taylor read a series of principles for carrying out the principles discussed at the previous meeting after which discussion arose and the meeting was adjourned for the discussion of the principles read by James Taylor by each separate paragraph. The Committee met on 29th December, 1851, and after discussing the principles read on a previous meeting the following resolutions were adopted:—

1st. That the two Societies to be called the Operative Plumbers and Glaziers Association.

2nd. That the object of this Association be to assist each other in cases of sickness, accident, death or trade dispute.

3rd.   That the expenses of sickness, accident and death or trade disputes be equalised on both Lodges according to their respective number of members.

4th.   That each Lodge after paying the proportionate share of expenses shall keep the overplus a fund for their own private use.

5th.   That each Lodge shall be governed by their respective officers and that a committee of three members from each Lodge with a Secretary be appointed to equalise the expenses and try all cases of dispute between either Lodges or their respective members.

6th.   That a uniform entrance fee be paid by the members of both Lodges.

7th.   That the hours of labour be adopted on the same principle by both Lodges.

8th.   That piece work shall not be allowed by any member of either Lodge.

9th.   That the members of either Lodge out of work shall be allowed to apply at either Club House for work.

10th. That the members of both Lodges shall have the privilege of visiting either Lodge at their respective meetings at pleasure.

11th. That a uniform payment be made to the members of both Lodges in case of sickness, accident, death or trade dispute.

12th. That the members of this Association shall not be allowed to slander or lessen the character of each other.

The Committee after adopting the aforesaid principles appointed Messrs. Taylor and Bell to wait upon the Peter Street Society on the 2nd January, 1852, and the Black Moors Head Society on the 17th January, 1852, to state the reasons for the committee coming to such conclusions and as they the committee had gone further than they were appointed they wished to have the opinion of the two Societies on their proceedings previous to forming detailed Rules on the above principles. Messrs. Taylor and Bell accordingly waited upon the two Societies and laid the aforesaid principles before them when the two Societies unanimously approved of the Principles read by Messrs. Taylor and Bell. The committee met again on 19th January, 1852, when Mr. Thomas Baley attended from the Peter Street Society in the place of Joshua Sidebottam who could not attend. Messrs. Taylor and Bell delivered their report from the two Societies when Messrs. Taylor, Smith and Baley were appointed as a sub-committee to draw up a code of rules in detail on the principles adopted by the two Societies, and to report the same to the committee. The committee met 2nd February, 1852, to receive the report of the sub-committee which after discussion the rules brought forward by the sub-committee were adopted and it was resolved that a General Meeting of the two Societies should be held at the Black Moors Head on Thursday, 12th February, 1852, for the purpose of discussing and adopting the rules brought forward by the committee.

A General Meeting of the two Societies was held at the Black Moors Head, 12th February, 1852, Mr. Joshua Side-bottam in the chair. After discussing the rules by each separate paragraph brought forward by the committee the following resolution was unanimously adopted.

1st. That the rules brought forward by the committee and read over separately with the alterations now made with the exception of the rule on the hours of labour do pass.

2nd. That this meeting recommends to the General Managing Committee when appointed to take into consideration the question of the hours of labour and report the same to a general meeting of the two Societies.

3rd. That James Taylor be the General Secretary.

4th. That the opening meeting of the General Managing Committee be held at the Black Moors Head on 25th February, 1852.

(Sgd.) JAMES TAYLOR,

General Secretary.

APPENDIX 2

April 1866

FELLOW MEMBERS,

The present report is submitted to your notice as the first report issued by the Association, it having only been in existence since December last, and in consequence, we have not got into proper working order; so that allowances must be made for any imperfections that may appear; trusting that as we proceed we may gain experience and improve, and that the Association may prove both useful and beneficial to all connected with it; and be the means of putting an end to disputes, and creating a better feeling between both employers and employees. We have this quarter opened two additional Lodges, one at Rochdale and one at Bolton, and I am happy to state that we have three more applications for opening Lodges, one at Newcastle upon Tyne, at Leeds and Stirling. I may inform you that it is at present under consideration at Dundee and Lancaster to ask for an advance on their present rate of wages, as they only receive 21s. per week; should there happen to be a dispute (which I do not think probable from the information I have received), I will send to each Lodge an account of the same, when all that choose can send aid, if required by them. Earnestly hoping that every member will use his influence and endeavour as far as lays in their power to strengthen the union; members knowing of any Lodges not in connection will oblige by giving the addresses so that they may be communicated with; with the view to their joining the Association.

With best wishes to all, allow me to remain,

Yours Respectfully,

J. H. DOBB,

8, Marquis Street, Liverpool.